Pigeon English

Gbolahan Obisesan is an award-winning playwright and director living in London. His previous plays include *How Nigeria Became: A Story, and a Spear that Didn't Work* (Unicorn Theatre, 2014) and *Mad About the Boy* (Edinburgh Festival Fringe, 2011), which received a Fringe First for Best Play. He was one of the six writers, and the only British writer, on Rufus Norris's *Feast*, commissioned by the Royal Court and The Young Vic for their World Stages London which was produced at the Young Vic in February 2013.

Stephen Kelman was born in Luton in 1976. *Pigeon English*, his first novel, published by Bloomsbury, was shortlisted for the 2011 Man Booker Prize, the Desmond Elliott Prize and the *Guardian* First Book Award, and he was also shortlisted for the New Writer of the Year Award at the 2011 Galaxy National Book Awards. *Man On Fire* was published by Bloomsbury in 2015.

Plays for Young People

Methuen Drama's *Plays for Young People* series offers an excellent selection of single plays and anthologies aimed at young people to perform. The series features the highest-quality work by established playwrights, which is age-appropriate and organised into age bands to help teachers and youth theatre leaders select the most suitable work for their group.

Gbolahan Obisesan

Pigeon English

Adapted from the novel by Stephen Kelman

Bloomsbury Methuen Drama
An imprint of Bloomsbury Publishing Plc

B L O O M S B U R Y
LONDON • NEW DELHI • NEW YORK • SYDNEY

Bloomsbury Methuen Drama

An imprint of Bloomsbury Publishing Plc

Imprint previously known as Methuen Drama

50 Bedford Square	1385 Broadway
London	New York
WC1B 3DP	NY 10018
UK	USA

www.bloomsbury.com

BLOOMSBURY, METHUEN DRAMA and the Diana logo are trademarks of Bloomsbury Publishing Plc

First published 2015

Pigeon English by Stephen Kelman
Copyright © Stephen Kelman 2011
Adapted for the stage by Gbolahan Lekan Obisesan
Copyright © Gbolahan Lekan Obisesan 2015

Stephen Kelman and Gbolahan Lekan Obisesan have asserted their right under the Copyright, Designs and Patents Act, 1988, to be identified as author of this work.

With thanks to Alice Downing for her contribution to the spoken-word pieces featured and, in particular, those spoken by the character of Never Normal Girl.

British Library Cataloguing-in-Publication Data
A catalogue record for this book is available from the British Library.

ISBN: PB: 978-1-4742-5103-7
ePDF: 978-1-4742-5101-3
ePub: 978-1-4742-5102-0

Library in Congress Cataloging in Publication Data
A catalog record for this book is available from the Library of Congress.

Series: Plays for Young People

Typeset by Fakenham Prepress Solutions, Fakenham, Norfolk NR21 8NN
Printed and bound in India

Preface

Upon first reading *Pigeon English*, I was immediately struck by how vividly I was able to immerse myself in the environment and how much of Harri's adolescent viewpoint resonated with me.

A lot of what I had read conjured up memories I had forgotten as an immigrant of Nigerian heritage. My own initial reaction when moving to London, with its many encounters and the city's myriad of cultures and people, had been similar to those of Harri, making the novel all the more poignant for me as I read.

Adapting the story for the stage was an immense challenge that I initially did not want to undertake. I felt that Stephen had created a mesmerising and enchanting narrative tapestry through the eyes of Harri and Harri's fascination with, and relish of, the discoveries around him. Therefore, a dramatic stage adaption would warrant sacrificing evocative passages and characters, distilling longer emotional discoveries, and maybe even clipping the wings of pigeons.

I soon reconciled all my trepidation with the fact that this was one of those stories that I emphatically wanted to lend myself to as best as I could and proceeded to work on my drafts.

Harri's journey from vulnerable innocence and romanticism to corruption and disillusionment, and his conscious effort to heal the wounds around him, felt the most pertinent themes for me to focus on and explore as I went forward.

As I proceeded, Harri's family and prominent friends, and those he wanted to accept him, were extremely important to the story and integral to what eventually became this adaptation meant for presentation on a stage.

The more challenging aspect of the work became the elements of the adaption that I felt were hindering the dramatic narrative of a play. I wrestled with which of the many young voices and school friends Harri occasionally references I could sacrifice for their less-than-'bo-style' contribution.

I endeavoured and really hope to have retained the glorious aspects of Stephen's novel and, with this stage adaptation, to have created a story for the stage with heart and youthful exuberance that stands the test of time. I hope that young and professional companies gravitate towards the piece with love and respect for the voices and the travails of the environment depicted.

Gbolahan Obisesan, 2014

Pigeon English

The stage adaptation of *Pigeon English* was originally commissioned by the National Youth Theatre and Bristol Old Vic, directed by Miranda Cromwell, and first performed on the 7 August 2013 at Bristol Old Vic with the following cast:

Chanelle/Auntie Sonia/Clipz	Chanelle Bernard
Mamma	Paris Iris Campbell
Never Normal Girl/Kylie/Lady	
Cop/Agnes/Voice/Smaller Kids	Alice Downing
Lydia	Hayley Konadu
Miquita	Lara Simpson
Dean	Brandon Cook
Julius/Harvey/Papa/Dizzy	Omar Currie
Harri/Dead Boy	David Johnsson
Killa/Chicken Joe	Eben Figueirado
Jordan/Asbo/Mr Frimpong	Joseph Langdon
Fag Ash Lil/Mr Tomlin/Newsman/	
Next Hoodie	Felix Pilgrim
X-Fire/Pastor Taylor/Kwadwo/Mario	Jamal Taylor
Connor/Nathan/Terry Takeaway/Suspect/	
Hoodie	George Webster

Textual Notes

Words of dialogue in [ ] can either be said or omitted

A dash (–) indicates an interruption or change in thought/intention in dialogue

A forward slash (/) indicates an interruption by another character so that lines might overlap

A series of dots (...) indicate a trailing off of thought or a delayed response

Characters

Agnes
Asbo
Auntie Sonia
Chanelle
Chicken Joe
Clipz
Connor
Cop
Dean
Dizzy
Dead Boy
Fag Ash Lil
Mr Frimpong
Harri
Harvey
Hoodie
Jordan
Julius
Killa

Kwadwo
Kylie
Lady
Lydia
Mamma
Mario
Miquita
Nathan
Newsman
Next Hoodie
Never Normal Girl
Papa
Pastor Taylor
Smaller Kids
Suspect
Terry Takeaway
Mr Tomlin
Voice
X-Fire

Scene One

March.

'POLICE LINE DO NOT CROSS' stretches across the space.

We hear the crash of thunder before rainfall – Lightning strikes and haunting faces stare out from various inhabited spaces on stage.

A squabble of young men playing basketball – Laughter – Taunting – A disagreement – A Fight – Shadows dart in and out of the space – Swift and playful with hints of menace.

Thunder crashes and the rain starts to fall.

A haunting frail figure drifts in out of the darkness.

Never Normal Girl Sitting pretty's pretty shitty when you're stuck in this city of self pity and loathing. And when it comes to freedom and adventure most people here they don't dare to dip a toe in, but as days go by. Full of lies, of self sacrifice and not looking twice at the sky that could be reached if they had just tried to fly.

Petty lies from blinkered minds are trivialities that make our world fall blind.

The neon sign of Chicken Joe's is brightly illuminated in the background.

Two young boys stand at the front of the stage.

Nearby is a shrine to mark the spot a young man has been killed. A woman in black stands solemnly. Her features undistinguishable, she seems almost complete consumed by her black clothes in mourning.

This woman is a shadow of herself.

The sounds of a bird's wings fluttering down to the ground.

Harri (*to* **audience**) If you cross the police line you turn to dust. The dead boy's Mamma was guarding the blood. The rain wanted to come and wash the blood away but she wouldn't let it. Look at that pigeon, It's so hungry for chop – It just walked straight through the blood –

Dean   I'll give you a million quid if you touch the blood.

Harri   You don't have a million quid.

Dean   One quid then.

Harri *bows his head. Eyes squeezed shut.*

Dean   What are you doing?

Harri   Trying to see if I can make the blood move –

Dean   As if –

Harri   Asweh – It happened before – where I used to live there was a Chief who brought his son back like that. It was a long time ago, before I was born. Asweh, it was a miracle.

Dean   Well it didn't work this time – not for you.

Harri *reaches into his trouser pocket and pulls out a bouncy ball.*

Dean   What's that?

Harri   It's my bouncy ball – I don't need it anymore –

Dean   So give it to me –

Harri   No I want to give it to the dead boy – anyway I have five more under my bed – have you got anything to give him?

Dean *generously looks around and picks up a pebble off the floor.*

Dean   This –

Harri   That doesn't count – It has to be something that belongs to you.

Dean   I ain't got anything – I didn't know we had to bring a present.

Harri *reluctantly digs into his other trouser pocket and pulls out a strawberry chewit and hands it to* **Dean**. **Dean** *tries to unwrap it.*

Harri   Don't eat it – Give it –

Harri *and* **Dean** *both place their gifts down at the shrine.*

Harri   Now we must cross (*he makes the sign of the cross in front of* **Dean**)

Dean *make the sign of the cross in front of* **Harri**.
They repeat the action, this time crossing themselves facing the shrine.

Dean   Are we done?

Harri   Yes –

Dean   I'll race you (*he runs off*)

Harri   That's not fair –

Harri *gives chase.*

Scene Two

A cacophony of estate sounds.

We hear children in a play park juxtaposed with distant police sirens.

A moped races through the estate.

Dogs yap, growl and bark.

The scribbling of a note pad.

Harri *and* **Dean** *find themselves in a line.*

Police Questions.

Harri   When I came home from school there were police outside the flats. There were two police cars and a hell of cops all looking in the bushes and bins like they lost something special. One of the cops was a lady. Asweh, it felt very crazy. She even wanted to be a man. She had the same cop clothes on and everything. She was asking the kids questions, nobody could go home until they'd been interviewed. It was brutal. I think lady cops are a very good idea. They just talk to you instead of hitting you all the time.

Dean   Have you got any leads?

Harri   She's not a dogcatcher.

Dean   Criminal leads, dumb-arse.

Lady Cop   We're working on it.

Dean   If we hear anything we'll text you. What's your number?

Lady Cop   Cheeky – *[you stay out of trouble].*

Lady Cop *exits.*

Harri *holds his breath and closes his eyes.*

Lydia   What are you doing?

Dean   Holding his breath and feeling my blood going round.

What would you do if your blood was going to run out in five minutes?

Lydia   How?

Dean   Just if – Harri –

Harri *opens his eyes.*

Harri   If I knew my blood was going to run in five minutes … I'd just fill that five minutes with all my favourites things. I'd eat a hell of Chinese rice and do a cloud piss and make Agnes laugh with my funny face, the one where I make my eyes go crooked and stick my tongue right up my nose. At least if you knew you could be ready. It's not fair otherwise.

Terry T *arrives with his energetic dog Asbo.*

Harri   (*excited*) Asbo –

Lydia   Don't talk to him – You know who he is?

Dean   Of course we do –

Harri   It's just Terry Takeaway and Asbo – (*clapping his hand at the dog*)

Lydia   He's a thief-man, that's why they call him Takeaway –

Asbo does a big sneeze and shakes a leg.

Harri *and* **Dean** *laugh.*

Harri   I didn't know dogs can sneeze

Asbo does a bigger sneeze that seems to have crept up on it and makes the dog arch his back and shake its leg.

Harri *and* **Dean** *laugh as* **Lydia** *hides behind them.*

Terry T   He's allergic to beer, innit.

Harri   He looks sad –

Terry T   He's alright – Wanna buy these? Proper copper worth a bundle.

Dean   What are we gonna do with a load of copper pipes?

Terry T   (*sarcastic*) I dunno. You could sell 'em.

Dean   Why don't you sell them?

Terry T   That's what I'm trying to do innit.

Dean   I mean why don't you sell them to someone what wants them.

Terry T   Alright son, cool your boots – I was only asking.

Terry T *leaving.*

Terry T   Asbo – come boy –

Harri   We weren't even wearing boots. Asweh, Terry Takeaway na dey touch.

It's because he drinks beer for breakfast.

Harri, **Lydia** *and* **Dean** *exit.*

Interlude.

A beatbox underscores.

Dell Farm Crew *intimidates the audience.*

Harvey *snarls at the audience.*

X-Fire   Yeah – what you gonna do – what you gonna do when we come for you. This the DFC.

Clipz   DELL FARM CREW.

X-Fire   This my dog Harvey –

Harvey barks.

X-Fire   My gun man Killa –

Killa *points gun fingers with both hands at the audience his thumbs move up and down to indicates firing bullets.*

X-Fire   My chopper Clipz –

Clipz *wideyed indicates slicing his own neck with his thumb.*

X-Fire   That loops youth Dizzy –

All stop.

X-Fire   Where's Dizzy? It don't even matter – (*beat restarts*)

I'm boss round these Endz –

My tag's written on everything – Word to the wise, don't come looking for it with us manz otherwise it's peak season and I'll make your world collapse, take everything you work for like the twin towers.

Furthermore I need a new phone –

X-Fire *scans the audience with his left gun finger and stops on his victim.*

X-Fire   Yeah – Imma come for yours – Oie you man let's bounce.

Scene Three

Home/Family

Papa *is on the phone, the long distance call makes his voice sound echoey.*

The moment a pigeon flies into the flat is played out simultaneously.

Harri *puts flour into his hands and slowly begins to stalk the panicked pigeon.*

Papa   (*on the phone*) Hello – Are you there?

Harri   A pigeon flew in the window.

Lydia   Hurry up. It's going to bite somebody.

Harri   Advise yourself – he only wants to get out.

Don't scream – you will scare him.

Mamma   Make am commot from this place –

Papa   What did you do?

Harri   Lydia na scared for skin.

Lydia   How! No I am not.

Harri   She na even shake like leaf.

Lydia   It wings dey make me crazy.

Harri   I go catch am.

Papa   You dey catch am?

Harri   I dey get him for hand – His feet na feel scratchy for my hand.

Lydia   Aie – Take am for outside –

Mamma   Make you wash your hands so you no catch bird flu –

Harri   I took a proper good look at him to remember his colours, then I let him out on the balcony and he just flew away. I didn't even want to kill it for pepper soup.

Harri *sets the pigeon free on the balcony.*

Papa   Good work – You are the man of the house until I escape. It's your duty to look after everything.

Harri   You're not going to be long are you Papa.

12   Pigeon English

Papa   Of course not –

Harri   Its only been two months since we left, I will only start
to forget their faces after one year. **Agnes** couldn't come with us
because Mama has to work all the time. Grandma Ama looks after
her instead. It's only until **Papa** sells the things from his shop, then
he's going to buy some more tickets and we'll all be together again.

Harri   Hello Agnes

Agnes's *response is echoed from the phone.*

Agnes   'O!'

Noticing his mother.

Harri   When Agnes says hello Mamma cries and laughs at the
same time, she's the only person I know who can do it.

Harri   Can you say Harri?

Papa   Not Yet, Give her time.

Harri   What's she doing?

Papa   Just blowing some bubbles. You better go now.

Harri   Ok. Come soon. Bring some Ahomka, I can't find any
here. I love you.

Papa   I lov….

Phone cuts off.

Harri   I hate it when that happens.

Scene Four

Jordan.

The flat balcony landing.

Jordan *has a scooter and he's trying to master a trick.*

Harri   Jordan doesn't go to school. He got excluded for kicking a teacher. Excluded means thrown out. I didn't believe it at first, but even his Mamma said it was true. Jordan's skin lighter than me because his Mamma's Obruni.

Jordan   My mum's trying to get me in another school but no one wants me innit. I don't even care man, school's shit anyway.

Harri   What do you do instead?

Jordan   Bear stuff – Play Xbox. Watch DVDs

Harri   Does your Mamma make you do jobs?

Jordan   No way. Why, does yours?

Harri   Sometimes –

Jordan   That's so gay –

Harri   Only the man's work. Locking the door, checking for invaders, things like that –

Jordan   It's still gay – You wanna see something –

Harri   Yeah – what is it?

Jordan *pulls out a knife with a green handle.*

Jordan   This is my war knife – When shit gets peak – I'll be ready – It's well sharp look –

Jordan *holds the knife near* **Harri***'s face and twists the blade around in the air.*

Harri   It has a green handle same as the knifes from Mamma's block.

Jordan   Try and get the same one as mine, then we'll be war brother innit –

Harri   No thanks. I don't really need one –

Jordan   What's the matter – Don't you wanna be brothers?

Silence

Jordan   Rarse, you should've seen your face man – You was shitting yourself man –

Jordan *puts the knife away.*

Harri   No I wasn't – You're not even funny –

Jordan   Yeah whatever – come run outs – You're it –

Jordan *and* **Harri** *chase each other around the estate touch a rectangular box with handle protruding from the side of a wall.*

Harri   We greeted the rubbish pipe for luck – It's traditions inside is metal and it smells like shit, it goes all the way down to hell.

Jordan *puts his head inside and shouts.*

Jordan   Bollocks!

Harri *copies* **Jordan**.

Harri   Bollocks!

The sound echoes as it travels down the pipe.

A lift door opens.

Jordan *takes a big breath in and deliberately flems up a big ball of mucus that he gobs onto the buttons of the lift.*

Harri *noticing someone approaching.*

Harri   Fag Ash Lil's coming – (*to* **audience**) Fag Ash Lil killed her husband and ate him in a pie. Everybody agrees. That's why she has crazy red eyes – Mad and watery – it's from eating human meat

Jordan *and* **Harri** *hold the lift doors as* **Fag Ash Lil** *lights a cigarette and enters the lift.*

Fag Ash Lil   That's kind of you –

Jordan   You're welcome –

Jordan *and* **Harri** *let the lift doors close and listen.*

Fag Ash Lil   Bloody hell.

Jordan   Bloody hell, bloody hell, stupid bastard.

Never Normal Girl *meekly appears.*

Harri   Jordan look –

Jordan   She's so fugly, she stinks of cum – I can smell her from here –

Harri   Never Normal Girl is always scared like a little rabbit because her grandpa sexes her. She lives with him and he sexes her everyday.

Jordan   Watch out she's dirty – proper grim – you touch her and she'll give you herpes – she carries all sort of diseases – touch her and you'll be itchy all over for like –

Harri   Why doesn't she tell or get her mama to clean her?

Jordan   Her mum's dead innit – It's just her and her Granddad –

Harri   Why doesn't she go to the police then?

Jordan   If she told them they'd take her granddad away and then she'd have nowhere to live – she'll just be bopping around begging to sex you –

Harri   I feel sorry for Never Normal Girl.

Jordan   Err you want her to have your baby – just look at her and that's it she'll be duffed up –

Harri   No – She's fugly and a creep

Harri   I wanted to say she could live with me except Jordan would tell everybody I loved her – [I don't]

Jordan   Err she's gonna try and play with us – Let's get out of here

Jordan *and* **Harri** *leave.*

Never Normal Girl   Who gives a shit about what's behind my eyes, only searching for their own peace of mind that they always seem to find at the top of my thighs.

And so if they say I'm going out to get laid now that although I'm not going home alone failings all part of my grand plan because it might mean I fall into the hands of someone who gives a damn.

But this time as I'm unzipped, soft lips and warm pink finger tips strip me slowly just from waist to head, and when I'm undressed your nose traces that shadow of my spine. Every line entwines me to you as I aspire to be someone's one and only heart's desire.

But the punch line is I drempt you up, and I have to admit it's not enough because when day time comes and imagination fails, I'm just back to chasing fairy tales.

Scene Five

Late Night.

Harri *stands on the family flat balcony alone.*

Harri   Mamma and Lydia were both snoring like crazy pigs.

I go on the balcony and wonder if Papa is holding you looking up at the moon the same as me. The helicopters were looking for robbers again. I love living on floor 9, you can look down and as long as you don't stick out too far nobody on the ground even knows you're there.

I was going to do a spit but then I saw somebody by the bins so I swallowed it back up again.

He was kneeling on the floor by the bottle bank. He was poking his hand under like he dropped something there. I couldn't see his face because his hood was up.

Maybe it's the robber – Quick, helicopter, here's your man. Shine your torchlight down there.

He pulled something from under the bin. It was all wrapped up.

The hooded figure unwraps the wrapping and unveiled is a shiny pointy object. It's a knife. The hooded figure wrapped the object up again and put it down his trousers.

Harri   The helicopter didn't even see him. He just ran away
sharp-sharp towards the river. He runs proper funny like a girl
with his elbows all sticking out. I bet I'm faster than him. I wanted
to keep watching for if something else happened, but I had to
greet the chief too bad.

Scene Six

In England/Words.

It's playtime at school.

Harri, Kylie, Dean and **Nathan** *are all exchanging sweets.*

Harri   In England there's a hell of different words for
everything.

Piss and slash and tinkle and drain the main vain mean all the
same – the same as greet the chief. There's a million words for a
bulla. When I came to my new school the first thing Kylie Barnes
said to me was –

Kylie   Have you got happiness?

Harri   Yes?

Kylie   Are you sure you've got happiness?

Harri   Yes –

Kylie   But are you really sure?

Harri   I think so

Kylie   You think so – You mean you don't know

Kylie *starts laughing.*

Kylie   Got ya – hook line and sinker.

Nathan   It's just a trick – She's not asking if you've got
Happiness, she's asking if you've got a penis. She says it to
everyone. It just a trick. It only sounds like happiness but really
it's Ha-penis

Harri   I have a penis – Kylie is just a confusionist. At least I didn't lose. I do have a penis. The trick doesn't work if it's true.

Dean *pulls out a packet of crisps and shares with* **Harri***.*

Harri   Do you think it's the dead boy's fault they chooked him? Do you think they'll catch who did it?

Dean   Don't bet on it, the coppers round here ain't got the skills. They should get CSI on the case, they'll crack it in no time.

Harri   What's a CSI?

Dean   They're like the top detectives in America, they know the best tricks and they can find the clues that no one else has even thought of. It's not just on telly, it's real.

Harri   We should be like CSI – Find out who murdered the dead boy –

Dean   (*excited by the idea*) Then we'll get the reward and the police will give us our own office –

Harri   That will be brilliant – Papa will be so proud

Clipz *suddenly snatches* **Harri***'s bag.*

Dean *is stunned and frozen with fear.*

Dizzy   Dash it on the floor man (*to* **Dean**) What you gazing at?

Dean   (*nervously*) Nothing my contacts are dry – I can't even close my eyes

Dizzy   Maybe I'll spit in them –

Dean   I'll go toilet – thanks for the offer –

Dean *exits.*

Clipz *throws the bag to* **X-Fire***.*

Harri *tries in vain to retrieve his bag.*

X-Fire   Do you want it?

Harri   Yes

X-Fire   What you gonna do for it? – Come here

Harri *tentatively walks towards* **X-Fire.**

Harri   He picked me. I felt quite sick but I had to listen. I even wanted to listen. I just had to stand still. He didn't like it when I moved. His breath smells like cigarettes and chocolate milk. I wasn't even scared.

X-Fire   What country you from anyway?

Harri   Ghana.

Killa   Do the feds have guns there? They do, innit.

Harri   Feds?

Clipz   Ha aha – He doesn't know what Fed's are –

Dizzy   Police – Po – Po –

Killa   Do you like Feds – Do you want to be a Fed – I hate *Po-lice*

X-Fire   You know when the knife goes in them you can feel where it hits.

If it hits a bone or something it feels disgusting man.

Harri   X-Fire was teaching me about chooking.

He didn't use a real knife, just his fingers.

(*Flinches*) They still felt quite sharp.

X-Fire   You're best going for somewhere soft like the belly so it goes in nice and easy, then you don't feel nothing. The first time I shanked someone was the worst man. All his guts fell out. It was nuts – too sick. Happened cause I didn't know where to aim yet, I got him too low down. That's why I go for the side now, under the ribs above the hips. Then you don't get no nasty shit falling out.

Killa   In Ghana you make you houses out of cowshit innit.

Harri   No we don't –

Killa   Yes you do – I seen it.

Harri   Killa didn't join in. He was just quiet. Maybe he hasn't chooked anybody yet. Or maybe he's chooked so many people that he's bored by now. That must be why he's called Killa.

Dizzy   The first time I chooked someone the blade got stuck. I hit a rib or something. I had to pull like some fassie to get the knife out. I was like, give me my blade back bitch.

X-Fire   Don't be a dickhead … Lil man's firming it still – Innit Ghana, you're kinda hard innit – Tell you what, you can have your bag back if you do a job for me.

Harri   I don't need a job. I just lock the doors at home and carry the heavy things for Mamma.

Killa   What's he chatting about? Lil man so comedian like that midget Kevin Hart – You hart-less lil man?

They all laugh.

Dizzy   Do you wanna roll with us – (*talks down to* **Harri**) If you roll with us we'll show you what's good –

Clipz   Rolling with DFC is a Hype still – Bare jokes –

X-Fire   We'll look out – back you innit –

X-Fire *hands* **Harri** *his bag back.*

X-Fire   Keep it real, Ghana. You get into any madness from any man, you come check for me – you understand?

X-Fire *grabs* **Harri***'s bag.*

Harri   Yes, please – Don't rip my bag – Or Mamma go make my ears ring –

X-Fire *lets go of* **Harri***'s bag.*

Harri *leaves.*

Lydia *walks with* **Miquita** *to Cafeteria steps.*

Miquita   Wasn't that you brother?

Lydia   I don't think so

Dizzy   (*to* **Lydia**) Where you going sweetness?

Miquita   None of you business – You're not invited –

Dizzy   I wasn't chatting to you –

X-Fire   Who's your girl?

Miquita   She's new –

X-Fire   I can see that – (*to* **Lydia**) What your name?

Miquita   Lydia – that's her name and we've got to go –

Dizzy   Why the fuck are you cock blocking?

X-Fire   Miquita fall back man – Oie new girl –

Lydia *finds the situation awkward and looks at* **X-Fire** *nervously.*

X-Fire   Lydie that's you're name yeah –

Lydia   Lydia – I prefer Lydia

X-Fire   You got a man?

Lydia *flattered and slightly caught off guard.*

Lydia   How! – Why? – What do I want with a man, I'm not a sugababe –

X-Fire   You look sweet to me –

Dizzy   Return of the Mac – Mac attack –

Clipz   Go in fam – move her up fam –

X-Fire   (*smiles*) Shut up – don't mind em idiots – so do you want a sugadaddy?

Lydia   No thanks – I have one dad and no one can replace him.

Clipz   Rejected rahhhs –

Dizzy   Don't have that fam – She ain't even all that –

X-Fire   Shut your mouth – that's cool – I like a challenge – I'll buk you up later still.

Lydia   What?

X-Fire   I'll see you later yeah –

Lydia   Maybe –

Miquita   Can we go now please?

X-Fire   Talk to your girl Miquita – I've got my eye on her –

Dizzy   Have a word with your girl Chanelle as well – Manz is roasting – I need her to free it up –

Miquita *and* **Lydia** *leaving.*

Miquita   I see what I can do but she Chanelle nah deal with no V-Reg –

Clipz   Pahhhhaaahhhh –

Dizzy   I ain't no virgin – I ain't no virgin –

Miquita   Whatever –

X-Fire   You feel better shouting that out blood –

Dizzy   How's she trying to boy man off like that though – I ain't a virgin.

Scene Seven

Art Class/Poppy.

Harri   In art Tanya Sturridge was absent and Poppy sat in her chair instead. Then Poppy was almost right next to me. She stayed there for the whole lesson, she didn't even move away. It made me go all hot. I couldn't concentrate because I wanted to see what Poppy was doing. She was painting her fingernails. She actually used the paint for pictures to paint her fingernails with. I watched her the whole time. I couldn't even help it. She painted one fingernail pink and the next fingernail green, and then the next one pink again, in a pattern. It took a very long time. She was very careful, she didn't make a single mistake. It was very relaxing. It made me feel sleepy just watching it. Mrs Fraser says inspiration for your mood picture can come from anywhere, from the world or inside you. I got my inspiration from Poppy Morgan's hair. I used Poppy's hair for my yellow. I only didn't tell her for if it ruined it.

Scene Eight

Auntie Sonia, **Mamma** *and* **Julius** *are in the Kitchen.*

Harri *sits with* **Lydia** *on the sofa in the front room watching the News on TV.*

Harri   Mamma always goes serious when she pays money to Julius.

Her hands go proper fast like there's dirt on the money and she doesn't want to get it on her fingers.

Mamma   It's all there –

Julius   Hold on –

Julius *recounts the money.*

Auntie Sonia   You know you can trust her – she's my sister

Julius   This is what I do – No preferences – You made me lose my count –

Julius *restarts the count.*

Harri   They haven't found the dead boys killer yet –

Newsman   Police are still appealing for witnesses –

Mamma *joins* **Harri** *and* **Lydia** *on the sofa.*

Harri   Mamma – What you think the Killer looks like?

Mamma   I don't know – He could be anybody –

Newsman   There has been a public outcry –

Harri   You dey think he be black or white?

Mamma   I no know Harri –

Harri   I go bet he be one Junkie for the pub

Newsman   [Is there a] solution to preventing such a tragedy in the future

Harri *distracted studies* **Julius**'s *behaviour.*

Mamma   Where you get that from? Lydia, why you dey tell him these things –

Lydia   How! I didn't tell him anything –

Harri   Julius nah cold as ice – He just be cool –

Mamma   What you dey know about cool?

Harri   Mamma he dey drive big Mercedes Benz like he be President –

Mamma   He no be President – You better look the other way when you sabi men like Julius –

Harri   But he dey get money and wears big rings – rings like musicians on MTV –

Lydia *changes the channel to MTV.*

Mamma   Lydia what have I told you about this channel – I don't want you listening to this sort of music

Interlude – The **Julius** *Song.*

Ensemble   Every man want to be like Julius

Auntie Sonia   Every gyal want a man like Julius. Know seh di man ah mi life name Julius, Julius, Julius

Julius *hits* **Sonia**.

Julius   Every man want to be like Julius,

Am a real boss man call me Julius

Mi jook up man because mi heartless

And mi jook up gyal because mi ruthless

Ensemble *sings chorus*   Every man want to be like Julius

Every gyal want a man like Julius

He's a real boss man call him Julius Julius Julius

Julius   Chicken Joes….

Ensemble   He supply that

Julius   Fries and a side …

Ensemble   that's a side that

Julius   DFC …

Ensemble   Him ah run that

Julius   Drugs and food …

Ensemble   Do you want that?

Chorus   Every man want to be like Julius

Every gyal want a man like Julius

He's a real boss man call him Julius Julius Julius

Mamma   No you cannot have a ring like Julius

Julius *bemused stands with* **Auntie Sonia**.

Julius   The count was fine – I'll be in touch.

Auntie Sonia   Please wait for me in the car – I'll be right behind you.

Julius   Don't be long – I've got things to do –

Auntie   Next time I go to America –

Mamma   Are you planning another trip then? You just got here.

Auntie Sonia   It's been six months.

Mamma   And your feet are itchy already?

Auntie Sonia   It's not my feet I'm thinking of.

Mamma   Are you taking care of your fingers?

Harri   Auntie Sonia burned her fingers to get the fingerprints off. Now she has no fingerprints at all. It's so if the police catch her they can't send her away. Your fingerprints tell them who you are. If you have no fingerprints, you can't be anybody. Then they don't know where you belong so they can't send you back. Then they have to let you stay.

Auntie Sonia   So you can see how black and cracked they are – It's just the best way to get by – You still enjoying delivering babies?

Mamma   Had a woman asking Janette are there any more midwives on the ward – And Janette ask her why.

Auntie Sonia   And why?

Mamma   She say's it's her first baby, do I know what I'm doing. She says she don't want no fuzzy-wuzzy just got off the boat.

Auntie Sonia   Fuzzy-wuzzy? That's a new one.

Mamma   I swear by God. I said I didn't come on a boat, I came on a plane. They have planes now where I come from. I shouldn't have said anything really. I had to apologies to her.

Auntie Sonia   How – You had to apologies? I would have rough her. I'd tell her I gave her a juju curse, her baby will come with two heads. She'd probably believe it.

Mamma   You can't say that, it's not professional.

Auntie Sonia   Fuzzy-wuzzy, I'll have to remember that one.

Harri   What's a fuzzy-wuzzy?

Mamma   It's what they call you when you're new at the hospital. Sometimes if you're new the patients doesn't trust you to do the job. It just means somebody who's new.

Harri   Why fuzzy-wuzzy though? I don't get it.

Mamma   I don't know. Don't disturb.

Auntie Sonia   It's for the noise the nurse's shoes make. When they're new they squeak on the floor. The noise just sounds like fuzzy-wuzzy that's all.

Harri   How come your shoes don't make that noise in here?

Mamma   It only works on shiny floors.

Auntie Sonia *hugs* **Mamma** *and* **Lydia**.

Harri   It sounded quite crazy. It could be true. Next time I get new shoes I'm going to try it. The corridors in the flats have proper shiny floors. I bet they'll make the dope-finest squeaking you've ever heard.

Auntie Sonia   (*hugs* **Harri**) Bye Harri –

Harri   Come back soon –

Scene Nine

Congregation is in full swing.

Singing a Ghanaian Church song – **Mr Frimpong** *sings loudly.*

Harri   Mr Frimpong is the loudest singer in Church, even if he's the oldest.

He just wants his voice to be the first one that God hears. It's not even fair. What if he sings so loud that God can't hear anybody else?

Lydia   He probably wears a tie in the bath.

Harri   Don't be disrespectful.

Lydia   Shut up, creep.

Mr Frimpong *is taken by the Holy-spirit and falls to the floor.* **Pastor Taylor** *goes to his aid on the floor and slaps* **Mr Frimpong** *across the face.* **Mr Frimpong** *gets up off the floor.*

Pastor Taylor   Praise God –

Harri   I think it was God who sent him asleep in the first place. He probably didn't like his singing anymore, it's too loud. That's why they put cages on the windows. It's not to stop the rogues throwing stones, it's to stop the windows breaking from Mr Frimpong's singing.

Pastor Taylor   Let us pray – Let us pray for Insight

Oh God I say Lord give our parents the strength to raise their children to be proper contributing members of society. Lord if any of the children are confronted with danger, protect them and give the voice to tell and inform the police of anybody with a knife. We ask that the dead boy's soul be carried into the arms of the Lord and the Lord soften the hearts of his killers so they'd give themselves up.

We pray for the dead boy's Mamma that she does not spiral into depression and she is supported and can get over the grief of such a tragic loss – for the police we pray that God will give them the insight to catch the killer.

Harri   What's insight?

Mamma   It means wisdom – It's is a great gift God has given us.

Pastor Taylor   In Jesus's name we pray.

All   Amen

The Church disperses.

Pastor Taylor *shakes their hands as the congregation leaves.*

Scene Ten

Outside a Pub.

Harri *stands with hands clasped in prayer.*

Dean *anxiously stands next to* **Harri**.

Dean   Can you do one for us not getting our heads kicked in –

Harri   We'll be alright, don't worry. They won't kill us today, they're too busy getting boozed – Let's just stay by the door and keep one foot on the pavement to be safe.

Dean   Try not to breathe it in – we could get all boozed up.

A drunk and unruly bunch of suspects begin to appear on stage and seem to form an animated police line up.

Harri   Everybody who went in or came out could be the killer – they all looked at us like a hungry vampire.

Dean   Who are we looking for exactly?

Harri   I don't know – I only saw one hand when he bent down to get the knife. It could have been a glove. I was quite far away.

Dean   What about him?

Harri   Too tall – Our man was shorter.

Dean   Roger that – Alright this one?

Harri   There was a man shaking the fruit machine making the lights come on and swearing, his eye looked deadly like he wanted to destroy everybody. Killers always have a quick temper. It's one of the signs of guilt.

Dean   We also have to look to see If he's got ants in his pants – talking too fast – If he starts looking around too much like he's lost something – Smoking too much and Crying too much as well as biting his fingers oh and spitting –

Harri   (*to* **Dean**) Could be him. What shall we ask him? Did you do it?

Dean   Don't be a retard, you can't just ask it straight out. You have to try and trap him. Ask him if he knew the victim and just see what his eyes do. If he looks away it means he's guilty.

Harri   Will you ask him? I'll be back up.

Dean   I'm not asking him. It was your idea, you ask him.

Harri   I'm not going in there. I'll wait until he comes out.

Dean   I knew you'd do this. I'm not waiting here all day.

The suspect steps outside to smoke a cigarette.

Harri *and* **Dean** *are frozen with fear.*

Suspect   What's up lads, you looking for someone?

Dean   We're just waiting for my dad.

Suspect   You don't want to hang around out here, there's too many arseholes about.

Harri   It's a trick – guilty –

Suspect *lights a cigarette.*

Harri   Cigarette another tell tale sign.

Do you know the boy who died?

Suspect   Do what?

Dean   The boy – the one who got stabbed. He was his cousin.

Suspect   No, I didn't know him.

Harri   Do you know who did it?

Suspect   I wish I did. These fucking kids, they need drowning at birth.

Dean   How do you know it was a kid who did it?

Suspect   It's always kids innit. You wanna stay away from all that shit Boys, it only ends one way. Be smart yeah?

Harri   We are.

Harri   He was going to blow smoke in our eyes. It was another trick to make us blind so we couldn't pick any clues up.

Suspect *leaves.*

Dean   They're never gonna tell us nothing. As soon as they know they're being interviewed they just mug us off. We're not gonna get anywhere by asking, we have to find out for ourselves.

Harri   How?

Dean   Surveillance and evidence, it's the only way. CSI-style, fingerprints, DNA. That shit don't lie. Come on we need to make plans.

Harri   Dean's the brains because he's seen all the shows. I'm going to have to wash all the beer smell off before Mamma gets home from work.

She says a man who smells of beer is a mess waiting to happen.

Scene Eleven

At the flat.

Miquita *visits.*

Harri *by the door, anxious.*

Harri   I don't know why Mamma has to work at night as well. It's not even fair. Why can't babies just be born in the daytime. I just wish Mamma was here so Miquita wouldn't keep coming round all the time. I not letting her in until she promised not to suck me off.

Miquita *knocks at the door.*

Miquita   Why you playing so hard to get?

Harri   Stop disturbing me –

Miquita   Don't be like that, Juicy Fruit. I'm sorry – I promise Ok –

Harri *unchains the flat door and unlocks the front door.*

Harri   I have the potato smasher behind my back for if I needed to chase her away.

Miquita *enters with* **Chanelle**.

Miquita   Taking so long for? – Lydia just come to the door next time – Your brothers over long

Harri   Miquita, Chanelle and Lydia are testing their costumes for the carnival. They are all parrots. You can only tell from the feathers. (*to* **Lydia**) You can't even get a pink parrot.

Lydia   Yes you can, I've seen it.

Harri   That's a flamingo. You can't get a pink parrot, I'm telling you.

Miquita   You can get a pink tongue though. Look – (*sticks out her tongue and wriggles it towards* **Harri**)

Harri   It was disgusting. If a girl has an earring in her tongue it means she's slack everybody agrees.

Miquita   Watch me dance – You like my dance moves innit –

Harri   Adjei (*he gets up and attempts to leave, heading towards his room*)

Miquita   Where you going Harri? – You gonna make your lips nice and soft for me? You wanna borrow my chapstick?

Harri   No thanks Pigface – I'd rather suck off my own behind.

Miquita   Don't be like that – My milkshake brings all the boys to the yard …

Miquita *dances on the table.*

Harri   Asweh, Miquita looks stupid in her costume. It makes her boobs look too close up like they're going to jump out and eat you. I even wish there was no such thing as boobs then you wouldn't want to squeeze them all the time.

Harri *leaves but spies from a doorway.*

Miquita *laughs and gets off the table, she grabs a small bag.*

Miquita   Now you're brothers out the way – Here's that thing –

Lydia   Why here?

Miquita   Because I can trust you – We're friends – You one of the crew –

Lydia   Can't you just deal with it –

Miquita   I won't ask you if I could – Check it –

Miquita *opens the bag and her and* **Lydia** *look inside.*

Miquita   You see – Please – I'll owe you one

Harri *steps out.*

Miquita *and* **Lydia** *are startled.*

Lydia   Harri! What are you doing?

Miquita   I'm going now –

Lydia   Oh ok –

Lydia *sees* **Miquita** *out.*

Harri   Lydia put the bag in the black sack with the washing. I pretend I didn't see.

Lydia *returns and goes to put on shoes.*

Lydia *grabs the washing bag and goes to the door.*

She pokes her head outside and checks that the coast is clear.

Lydia   Stay there, I won't be long –

Harri   Are you going to the Laundrette? I'm coming – I go beat you at the washing game again –

Lydia   Too late –

Lydia *shuts the door in* **Harri***'s face.*

Scene Twelve

Laundrette.

Lydia *is the only person in the laundrette.*

Lydia *takes out the content of the Nisa bag and put them in an empty washing machine.* **Lydia** *gets out a bottle of* **Mamma**'s *bleach from the washing sack and squeezes all into the machine, all over the things inside.*

Harri   The Laundrette is at the bottom of Luxemburg House, they're for everyone who lives in the flats.

Lydia did everything proper fast like it was a mission. Her hands were going so fast she couldn't even get the money in at first, then when the machine was going round she took the sack with the real washing still inside and …

Lydia *almost collides with* **Harri** *on her way out.*

Lydia   How! Why did you follow me? I told you to stay inside –

Harri   What was in the bag?

Lydia   Nothing –

Harri   I saw it already –

Lydia   I don't care – what is it then?

Harri   Just some stupid things –

Lydia   Don't bring yourself, you don't even know. It's only leftover bits from the costume – they were no good, we got paint on them.

Harri   I saw the things in the bag and they didn't belong to a costume, they were the wrong colour and the material wasn't shiny. It was boy's clothes. I saw the hood and the Ecko rhinoceros on the front.

There was red all over it. It was too dark for paint and too light for shito.

Lydia   It's not of your business – just go back inside –

X-Fire *arrives with Harvey.*

Harvey *pulling at his lead and licking his lips.*

X-Fire   Did anyone see you?

Lydia   (*glances at* **Harri** *briefly*) No –

X-Fire   Best get going Ghana – He's hungry innit.

Harri *keeping his attention on* **Harvey** *quietly starts to leave.*

Harri   **Lydia** are you coming?

Harvey *barks at* **Harri**.

Harri *scurries off.*

X-Fire   How long's it going to take?

Lydia   Maybe one hour –

X-Fire   You know what to do with it after that?

Lydia   Take it with some other old clothes to the Cancer Shop

X-Fire   When?

Lydia   Tomorrow?

X-Fire   Asap – Make sure its proper clean and don't chat to no one when you dump it at the shop –

Lydia   Yes

X-Fire   Yes what?

Lydia   I won't talk to anyone –

X-Fire   I like you – You know that innit – I like your brother – You guys are gonna fit in nicely round here – DFC will look after you – I will look after you –

Lydia   I should go – I'm not suppose to leave **Harri** on his own –

X-Fire   Wait – Come here –

Lydia   Yes –

X-Fire   Give me a kiss –

Lydia *tentatively kisses* **X-Fire**.

X-Fire *holds* **Lydia**'*s face in his left hand squeezing her cheeks.*

X-Fire   Just don't forget to take care of everything and I'll take care of you and your brother – You hear me?

Lydia   Yes – Thank you –

Scene Thirteen

Funeral.

A church bell rings out.

A dirge/procession juxtaposed with a Ghanaian funeral.

Everyone is wearing black.

Some people are under umbrellas to avoid the rain.

A camera crew is present with a female reporter.

Mamma *holds* **Harri** *and* **Lydia** *close and tightly.*

Harri   The dead boy's coffin was just normal except it had the badge of Chelsea on it. It still looked bo-styles. All his family were very sad. It felt proper dark because of the rain and all the black they were wearing.

Mamma   God rest him

Harri *sneaks away from* **Mamma** *and* **Lydia**.

Harri   I sneaked away from Mamma and Lydia, they didn't even know I was gone. Dean was waiting for me in the car park. We were spies. We watched the crowd for suspicious activity.

Dean   Sometimes the killer comes back to watch the funeral, he wants to rub the cops noses in it. It's like giving them the finger. He don't wanna get caught though, he's not that dumb. Look out for geezers with their hoods up.

Harri   Everyone's got their hoods up, it's raining cats and dogs.

Dean   Alright, and what colour hoodie was your geezer wearing? No forget that, he'll have dumped it by now. Think, Think.

Harri *has an idea.*

Harri I know, we could greet everybody and whoever doesn't shake our hand must be hiding something. We'll just go to shake hands because you have to at a funeral –

Dean With everybody? –

Harri With everybody and say congratulations and see who doesn't join in.

Dean Commiserations, not congratulations.

Harri Whatever. We'll just say sorry. Follow me.

Harri We pretended like we were the official greeters – Sorry

Dean Sorry

Hoodie Sorry.

Harri and **Dean** Sorry.

Hoodie *drops his cigarette and shakes* **Harri**'s *hand / Could happen as described in* **Harri**'s *text.*

Next Hoodie Sorry.

Harri *and* **Dean** *move along to next hoodie.*

Harri and **Dean** Sorry.

Hoodie You taking the piss.

Harri No, it's for commiserations.

Dean You got a problem with that?

Hoodie Fuck you, you cheeky little cunt.

Harri We were going to make him a suspect except it was the butcher and he was too fat to be the killer. He's just mean to everybody.

Scene Fourteen

Poppy *likes* **Harri***'s trainers.*

Harri   The number one best trainers are Nike Air Max. Everybody agrees. They're the most bo-style of all. Adidas is number two. Reebok's number three and Puma's four. Puma makes the Ghana kit.

My trainers are called Diadora. I got them from Nobby's shop in the market.

Everybody calls them pants but they're just vexed because they go faster than them. It even made a mighty squeaky sound. It does sound like fuzzy-wuzzy. It even works on Diadoras, not just nurse shoes. Poppy loves my Diadoras. She thinks they're bo styles. That's why we belong together, because we love the same things. We both love Diadoras and Michael Jackson. Sometimes I do the moonwalk for her or sing a song.

Harri *demonstrates his hilarious Michael Jackson medley with songs and dance moves.*

Scene Fourteen b

Dean   Nathan you have to run through the whole school shouting hairy bollocks.

Nathan   Minor –

Nathan *runs around flailing his hands hysterically.*

Nathan   Hairy bollocks

Harri   Nathan Boyd isn't scared of anything. We always try to think of a bigger dare for him to do. It always has to be bigger than before.

Nathan   That wasn't even a proper dare –

Kylie   You have to lick the crack spoon –

Nathan   What crack spoon? Where is it?

Harri   It's the spoon by the main gate. It's all bent and burned. It is the most disgusting spoon in the world.

Kylie   You have to put it all the way in your mouth – near your throat and suck it.

Nathan   I'm not sucking that, it's got crack on it.

Dean   Pussy

Nathan   Your Mum is – Can I wipe it first?

Kylie   No you have to suck it like that

Nathan   Why don't you suck it? You're used to sucking dicks.

Dean   Don't try and pussy out. You can't ask us to dare you and no do the dare.

Harri   You asked us –

Nathan   Fuck it then –

This almost happens in slow motion.

Harri   He just picked it up and licked the spoon

Nathan *licks the spoon and then throws it away.*

Nathan *heaves in disgust.*

Harri   I though he was going to puke, but he didn't

Kylie   That's wasn't even a suck, that was only a lick.

Nathan   You suck it then (*offers the spoon to* **Kylie**)

Kylie *flinches.*

Kylie   Nah you're alright

Nathan *offers the spoon to the others.*

Kylie *runs off pursued by Nathan leaving* **Harri** *and* **Dean**.

Harri   Nathan Boyd is the bravest in Year 7. It's even official. But even Nathan wouldn't dare to set the fire alarm off.

First Test.

Dell Farm Crew *still in school uniform are trying to be inconspicuous whilst they keep a look out,* **X-Fire** *and* **Dizzy** *instruct* **Harri**.

X-Fire   Ghana! – You sure you ready for this?

Harri   Yes –

X-Fire   You ain't gotta do it if you ain't got the balls.

Harri   If I was in the Dell Farm Crew Vilis couldn't abuse me anymore. If I wanted to swap my trainers the other person would have to do it and there will be no swapping back.

X-Fire   Just break the glass that's it– The alarm goes off –

Dizzy   Teachers don't want youths to burn so everyone gets an extra break –

Harri   What if it doesn't break the first time?

Dizzy   Just keep going till it does. We need to know you've got what it takes.

X-Fire   We'll back you up innit. I'll tell you if someone's coming.

X-Fire *and* **Dizzy** *point the fire alarm out to* **Harri** *and conceal themselves.*

Harri   Ok –

Harri *anxiously berates himself as he approaches the alarm.*

Harri   Hurry up, hurry up – sharp sharp.

X-Fire   Go on. Put some hustle in it.

Harri *bashes the fire alarm a few times to no avail.*

Harri's *hand begins to hurt and he flexes and massages his hand.*

Harri *presses the glass with his right thumb to no avail.*

Harri   I wanted a hammer. I wanted to run. I looked around for help but X-Fire and Dizzy were gone, all I could hear was them

Distant laughs.

Dizzy   (*shouts*) Pussy boy!

Harri   My belly felt proper sick. I think the Dell Farm Crew are enemies now. That's what happens when you fail your mission. Adjei, my hands are too soft for everything.

Scene Fifteen

Harri *and* **Dean** *getting tangled up in Sellotape.*

Dean   Sellotape can do lots of different detective jobs. You can catch fingerprints in it or hairs. You can use it to make traps. You can stick your notes down so they don't blow away.

Harri   You can even catch the criminals themself if you have enough, like if you made it into a spiderweb. Only it would take all sellotape in the world to hold a fully grown person. We tested it first with our fingerprints. It worked a treat. You could see all the tiny patterns. Everyone's patterns are different.

Dean   Sweet – I told you it'd work.

Harri   We were going to check the murder scene first -

Dean and **Harri**   Chicken Joe's

Scene Fifteen b

At Chicken Joe's.

Chicken Joe   Get out of it, you little sickos – Have some fucking respect – This is a business not a playground –

Harri and **Dean**   We've got respect, we've got respect – We're only helping.

Chicken Joe   Fuck Off before I call the coppers –

Dean   Your chicken's rancid anyway – It's got maggots in it.

Harri   We'll check at the river instead.

Dean   Let' split up to make it go faster –

Harri   You just had to stick a piece of sellotape on every surface that the killer might touch. If any fingerprints got stuck it meant the killer was there.

Dean   If you can match a fingerprint from where the boy was killed to one from where the knife was hidden it means whoever you saw must be the killer.

Harri   Dean knows what he's talking about, he's seen all the shows.

Dean   No luck – Swap –

Harri   Yes – Dean was the lookout while I looked for footprints like on CSI.

I was very careful. It felt lovely searching. It made everything go quiet like you were on an important mission and you were the only one who could fix it.

Dean   See anything?

Harri   Nope –

Dean   He's probably covered his tracks. And it's been raining. All the evidence probably got washed away. We just need to find some more leads, that's all.

Harri   What will you buy with your half of the reward?

Dean   A Playstation 3 probably – and a new bike and a shitload of fireworks.

Harri   Me too – Dean's the best partner a detective can have, he knows all the tricks. I don't even care if he cries when he watches Happy Feet. That's just means he cares.

Scene Sixteen

Dean *jumps on a wheelie bin and climbs onto a garage roof.*

Dean *on the roof.*

Dean   Come up, it's alright. I'll pull you.

Harri   You sure it's safe – We won't fall through –

Dean   Stop being a girl –

Harri   Hey – Ok –

Dean *helps up* **Harri**.

Harri   This is so cool –

Dean   What's this?

Dean *picks up a wet and oily parcel wrapped in a torn up cloth.*

Dean   Shall I open it?

Harri   Open it –

Dean   Do you really want me to open it though? What if it's anthrax or human teeth?

Harri   Just stop vexing me and open it –

Dean *unwraps the parcel to reveal a blue wallet with black velcro.*

Harri   Is there any money?

Dean   Hang on, it's all sticky.

Dean *opens the Wallet.*

Dean   Nah it's empty – There's something here though –

Dean *peels the piece of paper off an inside pocket of the wallet. It's a photograph.*

Harri   That's the dead boy –

Dean   Do you reckon?

Harri   I swear by God – He's even got his Chelsea shirt on.

Dean   You hold the wallet – Is that his girlfriend?

Harri   I didn't even know he had a girlfriend

Dean   Do you think she was crossed eyed or is she just doing it unpurpose –

Dean *shows* **Harri** *the photo.*

Harri   I think It's a joke – What do you think the sticky on the wallet could be?

Do you think it's blood?

Dean   It looks like it or maybe oil. Oh (*excited*) There might be a fingerprint in there somewhere. Let's take it back to you house and go over it with sellotape.

Scene Seventeen

Seeing Auntie Sonia at her place.

Auntie Sonia, **Mamma** *and* **Lydia** *have plates in hand eating in separate corners of the flat.* **Harri** *also has a plate.*

Harri   Auntie Sonia lives in a house with two flats. Her flat is down stairs. Everything in her flat looks brand new. Auntie Sonia even has a tree inside a pot. It's only tiny. A tree inside felt crazy, I didn't like it. I was worried for when the tree got bigger and hit the roof. Then it would die.

Auntie Sonia *drops her spoon on the floor.*

The sounds echos round the room loudly.

Auntie Sonia *is embarrassed.*

Harri   Is it because of your fingers?

Mama   Harrison!

Auntie Sonia   It's Ok – they're not babies, they should know.

Lydia   I want to know – You're always keeping secrets from us.

Mamma   Lydia

Lydia   It's true – Mamma does keep secrets. I found her lottery tickets, Mamma always says the lottery's for foolish people and you might as well throw the pound down a well.

Auntie Sonia   Where's the harm? I don't want to lie to them.

Mamma *breathes in heavily and collects the plates to wash in the kitchen.*

Auntie Sonia   There's nothing to it really. You just keep your fingers on the stove until all the skin has burned away.

Harri and **Lydia**   Did it hurt?

Auntie Sonia   It's quite scary the first time. You can smell your skin cooking. You have to pull your fingers off before they get stuck for good. It's the only time I cried.

Harri   I felt sick when I thought about it.

Auntie Sonia   You hardly feel it really – it's easier when you're boozed. Like most things –

Mamma   Don't tell them that –

Lydia   Do they feel funny?

Harri   They look funny – Auntie Sonia's fingers are all black at the end and shiny. It looks like it hurts. It looks like a zombie's finger.

Auntie Sonia   Sometimes – I can't feel the close-up of things anymore.

Lydia   Like what things?

Harri   Here – (*offering* **Auntie Sonia** *the TV remote control*)

Auntie Sonia   The buttons are too small.

Harri   She wasn't lying.

Lydia *pulling at her top.*

Lydia   Feel this pattern on my top.

Auntie Sonia *concentrates very hard as she feels the material and pattern on* **Lydia***'s top.*

Harri   It wasn't working, you could tell.

Mamma   That's enough now – leave her alone, she's not an animal at the zoo.

Lydia   Adjei, I don't know how you could do it – I could never do it.

Auntie Sonia   You do what you have to –

Mamma   You didn't have to do that.

Auntie Sonia   I thought I did at the time – This is where your Mamma and me will never agree.

Mamma   It's not the only thing.

Auntie Sonia   I did it the easy way. Some people do it with a lighter or a razor. It takes donkeys hours that way. Just get it over and done with, that's what I did. I'll stop burning them when I find the perfect place.

Harri   It could be here –

Auntie Sonia   It could be – we'll see –

Julius *returns with a baseball bat but no ball.*

Harri   Julius calls his bat the Persuader. He always brings it home from work with him.

Julius   He earned his keep today – Give him his bath, eh?

Julius *pats and whispers to the baseball bat before handing it to* **Auntie Sonia**. **Auntie Sonia** *takes the bat.*

Julius *goes to a cabinet to pour himself a glass of whiskey.*

Auntie Sonia   I'll wash it in the kitchen.

Julius   (*offering his whiskey glass*) Harri, want some?

Harri   No thanks –

Julius   The only friends a man needs, his bat and a drink. One to get you what you want, the other to forget how you got it. You'll see what I mean one day. Just stay good for as long as you can, eh? Just stay the way you are.

Harri   I will –

Scene Eighteen

Hair Straightner.

Lydia *has her head tilted back onto an ironing board.*
Miquita *is ironing* **Lydia***'s hair.*

Miquita   The detective don't get a gun though. The bad guy does – And he don't have to ask for what he wants, he just takes it. The detective's just an employee with a target on his back. I don't want to work for no one, man.

Harri   I bet your hair goes on fire.

Lydia   How! – No it won't

Harri   I bet it does

Lydia   Don't disturb.

Harri   I can watch if I want

[**Lydia** can't stop me watching. I'm the man of the house.]

Lydia   (*to* **Miquita**) Just don't burn me, Ok?

Miquita   Don't worry man. I've done it enough times.

Chanelle   Twice.

Miquita   So? I'm well skilful still. My auntie taught me, she learned it in Jail.

Harri   Miquita's auntie was a forger. It's when they buy something with a ticket except it isn't a real ticket, they actually drew it themself.

The whole thing takes donkey hours.

Lydia *is visibly rigid with concern of the iron. She closes her eyes tight shut as it gets closer to her face.*

Lydia   Watch my ears.

Miquita   Why – what are they doing?

Lydia   Don't mess around –

Harri   Lydia's hair was actually going flat. It happened right before our eyes. It looked bo-styles.

Lydia *enjoys the progress as her hair begins to straighten. She studies her new look and cheerfully smiles at herself in a hand mirror.*

Harri   You want to kiss yourself. Go on, kiss yourself.

Lydia   Don't disturb

Miquita   Keep still man or I'll burn you.

Miquita *holds the iron right next to* **Lydia***'s ear. The steam from the iron bellows out.* **Miquita***'s face changes to something more threatening.*

Miquita   Are you with us?

Lydia   What are you talking about?

Miquita   You know what I'm talking about. You're either with us or against us innit.

Harri   The iron was right over Lydia's eye. It was nearly touching it. The smoke was going in her face. My belly went cold. Chanelle ate the last Oreo.

Chanelle   Don't man, that ain't necessary. She knows the score innit.

Miquita   Shut up – Don't make me bounce you. You didn't see nothing – You don't know nothing right?

The actions seems to slow down as **Miquita** *taunts* **Lydia** *by moving the iron up and down menacingly.* **Lydia** *is visibly fearful.*

Harri *is also anxious for* **Lydia**.

Lydia   Please, I don't know anything. I'm with you, I'm with you.

Lydia *opens her eyes as* **Miquita** *moves the iron away.*

Lydia *checks her face in the hand mirror. She meticulously inspects her face.* **Miquita** *resumes the casualness of the earlier conversation as if nothing has happened.*

Miquita   Keep looking to the front yeah? It's gonna look well sick believe. Just keep still, I don't wanna hurt you. You shouldn't have moved.

Lydia   Sorry –

Harri   How! – It looks stupid. You look like a buffalo. [Telling a girl they look nice means you love them too much].

Chanelle   No it don't, you look wicked.

Miquita   I'm too good – I can't help it.

Harri   I got their finger prints on a piece of sellotape. [Chanelle gave me hers straight away but Miquita wouldn't cooperate. Then I remembered what Dean told me].

Dean   If they won't give you their finger, just get them to have a drink. Then the fingerprint will be on the glass. It's a piece of cake.

Harri   Miquita thinks she's so clever. Who's laughing now? I didn't need Lydia's fingerprint. She's not a suspect, she's just my sister. She didn't even cry when the burning came true.

Scene Nineteen

A Ghanaian barber, **Kwadwo**, rides his bike with a radio across the stage. He offers the audience his services.

Kwadwo   Bring your crusty head – You – yes you – Low cut – High cut – Kid n Play – Mike Tyson – Mohawk – David Beckham

any style – I can do it – When you make up your mind – Find me
– I am easy – I am loud –

Kwadwo *rides off on his bike.*

Harri   We couldn't see a barber on a bike, I don't think they
have them here. Kwadwo was my favourite barber where I used
to live, his bike had a radio as well. Here we have to go to a shop
instead. The barber was called Mario. He's quite grumpy.

Mario *walks on and his phone rings.*

Mario   Hold on – Sit down and don't move – mi haf fi take dis –
soon come

Harri   When he moved my head it was too rough. He did it too
fast. And his fingers were too hairy.

Mario   Mi na wan talk na man – Mi want curry goat – How
you mean you na write it down – take it again – (*as he walks off*)
Plantain / Rum punch

Harri   He even hates cutting people's hair.

Dean   He's only a barber so he can sell all the old hair to China,
they make it into clothes, innit.

Harri   Mamma can I have cornrolls.

Mamma   Why, so you can look like a bogah?

Harri   No I just like it – It's bo-styles –

Lydia   He only wants cornrolls because Marcus Johnson has
them.

Harri   Gowayou – No I don't

Mamma   Who is Marcus Johnson?

Lydia   He's in Year 11 – He thinks he's the ironboy – They
get the younger ones to do tricks for them – they have them all
running around. It's very sad. He calls himself X-Fire.

Harri   It's not X-Fire fool – It's crossfire – It only looks like
X-Fire when he paints it on the wall.

Lydia   Whatever – it's still sad.

Harri   Is not – At least nobody tells him what to do all the time, not like you keep making me kill the bedbugs – smash you own bedbugs, they don't even go on me.

Lydia   It was only one time – what are you saying? Are you saying I'm dirty?

Harri   One went up your nose when you were asleep – I saw it with my own two eyes. He's probably built a house in your brain by now. He's probably planted a garden and bought a satellite dish – he go live there forever.

Lydia   Gowayou!

Mamma   Stop vexing your sister – Your hair's not long enough for cornrolls anyway. You can have low hair – and don't make squeeze eyes at me.

Mario *returning.*

Mario   Yes so what you want –

Harri   I just want low hair –

Mario   You mean a number one or number two?

Harri   low hair –

Mario   Kanye West or Tupac

Harri   I swear by God – It was the funniest thing I've ever heard. Mario is dey touch. From today onward going I'm saving up all me hair until it's long enough for cornrolls, I don't care what Mamma says. Then I'll have the blood to pass any mission and they'll have to let me join the gang.

Scene Twenty

Carnival.

There is a jubilant atmosphere.

Everyone from the Dell Farm Estate is there.

It's raining.

Harri   Today was the carnival. It was raining cats and dogs but everybody still came. The dancer were so bright it still felt like the sun was out. There were djembes. You had to dance, you couldn't help it. Even the white people and the old people were dancing. The Never Normal Girl was next to me. She did a little baby dance. She was hardly moving at all. You only knew she was dancing if you looked at her feet. I felt sorry for her. I wanted to teach her a real dance but there was no time, I'd miss all the fun things. Asweh, It was brutal.

Harri   Agnes would love this! I could learn juggling for when she comes.

It was time for dance club. They were all parrots. Lydia kept forgetting to smile. She was too busy concentrating on the getting the moves right.

Harri   / Go Lydia –

Mamma   (**Mamma** *with camera*) Come on Lydia – Give us a smile.

During the dance presentation **Lydia** *slips and falls on the floor.*

Harri *is surprised.*

Mamma *is shocked and makes her way towards* **Lydia** *through the crowds.*

Lydia *is embarrassed and slowly hops off the stage.*

X-Fire *is on the side of the stage and puts a cold bottle of water on* **Lydia***'s ankle.*

Lydia *is surprised but appreciates the gesture.*

Smaller Kids   Pissy pant – pissy pants

X-Fire   Dock out before I clap you –

Lydia   Thank you –

Mamma   Ah Lydia – Move away from that vagabond – What are you doing with my daughter? Go and get a hair cut – Lydia where are going –

Lydia   Mamma you're so embarrassing –

Harri *takes opportunity to have a dance solo, enjoying himself as the carnival whines down.*

Scene Twenty-one

Costume.

Lydia *is cutting up her dance costume with scissors. Occasionally she would stop to pray.*

Harri *walks into the room.*

Lydia   Happy now?

Harri   What are you doing?

Lydia   What does it look like? You wouldn't believe it wasn't blood.

You think I'm a liar. Do you believe me now?

Harri   Don't you want to keep it? I thought you loved it.

Lydia   No I don't – It's stupid. I hate dance club anyway. It's stupid.

beat   Help me –

Lydia and **Harri** *scatter pieces of her costume off the flat balcony.*

Harri   We watched them fall like big snow rain. There were some smaller kids down below. They picked them up and made them back into feathers. They chased each other with them like crazy parrots.

Lydia   Don't tell anyone what I did will you?

Harri   Do you know who it came from?

Lydia   No, I swear to God. All I did was take the clothes to the launderette, that's it. It was only a test.

Harri   We kept watching until the smaller kids gave up and threw the feathers down. All the landed pieces looked like dead bodies just asleep. I said sorry inside my head but it wasn't sad anymore, it was strong.

Scene Twenty-two

Spit Sample/Stoning the Bus.

Harri *and* **Jordan** *are on a corner by the bus stop.*

Harri   Jordan was the first choice for a spit sample because he loves spitting so much. It wouldn't even be hard to get a sample, he'd just give it to me straight away.

Harri *holds out his sample pot.*

Jordan   F – off man, I ain't spitting in that.

Harri   It's clean –

Jordan   I don't care What you want me to spit for anyway – what you gonna do with it?

Harri *bites his lips to prevent him from smiling.*

Harri   It's for a science project, to test how well germs survive in spit. You get loads of different spits and you put the germs in them and the spit that kills the germs first is the special one. You could have a cure for something in your spit. It could make you loads of cheese.

Jordan   I don't wanna be a cure – let 'em die – I don't give a F – Just get it away from me man.

Harri *turns and throws the bottle in a nearby bin.*

Harri   Another idea bites the dust. Adjei, nobody wants to help the investigation. It makes you feel like everybody's the bad guy except you. It's very lonely. I haven't even got a favourite gun yet. If I had to choose, it would probably be a supersoaker – they sell them at the market. It's proper brutal. You have to ask the person for permission before you soak them for if they don't like water, otherwise there'll be a ruckus. I'm going to get one in the summer holidays.

Jordan   If I get a gun, it would be a Glock – It's what all the toughest gangsters use. Have you seen it?

Harri   No – what's it like?

Jordan   It's the sickest man. It the most powerful. If I shot you with a Glock it'll take your head off. It shoots dumb-dumbs innit.

Harri   What the hell are they?

Jordan   They're special bullets that can go through walls and everything. It's well deadly. That's the first gun I'm gonna get when I've got the cash.

Harri   Me as well –

Jordan   You can't have a Glock, it's mine. You don't even know about it till I told you.

Harri   I still love it –

Jordan   Yeah, well not as much as me. I love them the most – I've seen a Glock in real life too –

Harri   You lie –

Jordan   I ain't a liar – I have – DFC gave it to me – I had to hide it for them –

Harri   When – Why – how?

Jordan   They always keep a gun buried somewhere for when they need it. They've got loads of them all over the place innit –

Harri   Why don't they just keep it in their house?

Jordan   Don't be a retard – what if the police found it?

Harri   Did you shoot it?

Jordan   No, there weren't no bullets in it. You keep the bullets somewhere else, you don't keep 'em with the gun. I still fired it though. I pulled the trigger and everything. It was sick.

Harri   Jordan loved it, you could tell.

Jordan's *eyes bulge with excitement.*

Jordan   You've gotta be well quick though – if you're followed it's game over, DFC will kill you for giving the hiding place away. I only done it two times.

Jordan *looks out for the bus.*

Harri   Asweh, planting a gun just felt too crazy – At least if you're planting plants they'll grow into something. A gun doesn't even grow into anything. It was very funny. Planting a gun is the craziest thing I've ever heard of, I swear by almighty God.

Jordan *returns.*

Jordan   You should always know where to find a gun if you're in a hurry, you never know when you'll need it. You'll mostly need it for a war or to do a robbery with. It makes the robbery easier. If they see a gun they won't give you no shit innit, they'll be so scared they'll give you whatever you want. It's easy man. I can't wait to shoot someone though man. I'd shoot them in the face innit. I wanna see their head explode, that'd be wicked. I wanna see their eyes pop out and their brains splash all over the place.

Bus

Harri   The bus was coming we got ready. I had my stones in both hands. I waited for Jordans's command. You're not allowed to run until you've thrown all your stones.

Jordan   Now!

Harri   We jumped out.

Jordan *and* **Harri** *throw stones.*

Harri   I threw all my stones together. I didn't even aim them, I just threw them as fast and as hard as I could. The first one missed but the second one hit the side and bounced off. There were people getting off the bus. They didn't even try to stop us.

Jordan   Fuckers!

Harri   I only went cold when I saw Mamma coming. She was getting off the bus.

Mamma *spots* **Harri**.

Mamma   Harri! –

Jordan   Leg it.

Harri   We just ran. I was too scared to turn around. I wanted to puke. I didn't stop until we got to the tunnel.

Harri *and* **Jordan**, *breathing heavily, try to catch their breaths.*

Jordan   All mine hit. One on the window and one on the edge – a couple on the side. What about yours?

Harri   I don't know – One on the side I think, that's all.

Jordan   You're shit man – I win.

Harri   My stones were too sharp – that's the only reason.

I don't even care – I don't even need the points that much.

Harri *and* **Jordan** *step out.*

Mamma *is there waiting.*

Mamma   Ho – what do you think you're doing? Tell me I didn't just see that – what do you have to say?

Harri   Sorry, Mamma –

Mamma   You stupid boy – I go sound you – Get yourself home right now.

Mamma *grabs and pushes* **Harri** *towards the flats.*

Jordan *is amused by the encounter and begins to laugh at* **Harri** *and* **Mamma**.

Mamma   And you'll stay away from this boy.

Harri   It was an accident – we were only playing around.

Mamma   He's a waste of time – If I see you around this boy again there'll be big trouble.

Harri *looks back at* **Jordan**.

Jordan *spits in* **Harri**'s *face*.

Jordan   There's your sample pussy boy.

Jordan *sticks up his middle finger to both* **Mamma** *and* **Harri**.

Harri *wipes his eye with his sleeve*.

Harri *indiscriminately screams*.

Harri   Fuck off !!!!

Mamma   What did you just say? I go sound you and put pepper for your bottom.

Mamma *hits* **Harri** *on the back of the head*.

Mamma   Don't ever let me hear that word coming from your mouth again. I don't need your nonsense. Advise yourself Harrison. Have a think about what you've done or I go send you back to Ghana and you can explain yourself to your father.

Harri   I know what I did, I ruined everything. It's all broken and it's my fault. I knew it was true, I could feel it deep down. I should have done good. I should have been good but I let myself forget and now God's going to destroy us. He'll probably kill Agnes first just to teach me.

Scene Twenty-three

DFC Graffiti on the Jubilee Centre/Church.

Harri, **Mamma**, **Lydia**, **Mr Frimpong** *and* **Pastor Taylor** *stand outside the Jubilee Centre*.

Harri   There was no church today because of the broken glass and the bad words. Mr Frimpong was nearly crying. He loves church the most from all of us.

Mamma *gives* **Mr Frimpong** *a hug.*

Mr Frimpong's *body seems enveloped by the embrace.*

Mr Frimpong   It's senseless, that what it is – No respect for anything.

Harri   I was even glad at first, I'm tired of singing the church songs. It's just in the Jubilee Centre, in the room in the back behind the Youth Club. It's only a church on Sunday, the rest of the time it's just for bingo and old people's stuff. Everybody wanted the wet patch on the roof to be Jesus, but really it just looks like a hand with no fingers

Mamma   What is DFC?

Mr Frimpong   Who knows – Some code of theirs – Just nonsense.

Harri   I didn't tell them what DFC really means – I pretended not to know.

Mr Frimpong   Will they be on CCTV?

Pastor Taylor   They'll have covered their faces – they're ignorant but they're not stupid.

Harri   That's why Mamma won't let me get a hoodie, for if I cover my face. I don't even want to cover my face – I only want to keep my ears warm.

They tried to make it look like they put shit on the window but you knew it was only snickers.

Harri   We could go to the real church, the one where the dead boy had his funeral. It's only around the corner.

Mamma   It's the wrong kind of church.

Harri   How?

Mamma   Just because – They sing different songs – They're not the songs we know.

Harri   We can learn them – They might be better

Mamma   They're not better – We don't know them.

Harri   But I don't get it – It even a real church – they had the dead boy's funeral there – It must be good.

Mamma   It's just the wrong kind, that's all.

Mr Frimpong   Catholics – they want to give all of us Aids by telling people not to wear condums, so they can steal our land back again – It's true.

Harri   It has a cross and everything. It must be the right one if it has a cross. Do you want me to get my binoculars? They're only at home. Then I can look for clues.

Pastor Taylor   That's alright, Harri. I'll just clean this up.

Harri *turns to* **Lydia**.

Harri   If I was in the gang I could tell them about God. I could even save them. A gang can be for good things, not just for tricks. I could pass on the message.

Lydia   Just stay away from them, they're trouble.

Harri   What about Miquita, she's even worse. She's always trying to suck me off and you don't even stop her.

Lydia   That's different. It's different for girls, you don't understand. You need the right friends or they'll just rough you. Miquita's only bluffing, you can't take her serious.

Harri   If God saw what you did he'd take your eyes. I'm not going to be your guide dog when you go blind. I'll just pull you around on a string, it's your own fault if you can't keep up. I've got places to be, I'm not waiting for you.

Lydia   Don't bring yourself, Harrison. It was Miquita's blood, Ok?

Harri   How did her blood get there? She wasn't even cut.

Lydia   It's not that kind of blood. It's girls' blood. You don't know what you're talking about – Just go away.

Harri   You wouldn't have to cry if you weren't such a big liar –

Lydia   Just F – off

Scene Twenty-four

Confession.

The boys seem to be playing an elaborate version of hopscotch.

Harri   Nathan Barnes stood on a crack. It's bad luck. He did it on purpose, he just jumped right on it. The summer holiday will be ruined and it's Nathan Barnes fault.

They all punch **Nathan** *on the arm.*

Nathan   I don't care man –

Kylie   You dick – What'd you do that for?

Nathan   Cause I felt like it – so what? There's not really a spell – it's just bullshit –

Kylie   You're bullshit –

Nathan   Yeah, well – I know something you don't – I know who killed that boy.

Kylie   What boy?

Nathan   The one who got stabbed outside Chicken Joe's who'd you think – I saw it happening.

Harri   For real?

Nathan   For real – I was driving past – I seen the kid get stabbed and seen Jermaine Bent running away. I saw the knife and everything.

Kylie   Why didn't you tell the cops then?

Nathan   F – off, I ain't getting stabbed – they can do their own dirty work –

Kylie   I don't believe you – Whose car were you in.

Nathan   My brothers –

Kylie   What car's he got?

Nathan   A beemer – Five series –

Harri   That's when we knew he must be lying. Nathan's brother can't have a BMW, he isn't even rich enough. Nathan only wears Reebok Trail Burst.

Kylie *starts sniffing the air.*

The rest notice and prepare themselves.

Kylie   I can smell something – can you smell something? What is it – dogshit? No it's not dogshit. Cowshit? No hang on – It could be horseshit?

Nathan   Just F – off man –

Kylie   I know what it is, It's bullshit –

Harri   I couldn't believe it, it was too hard. I kept hoping there was another Jermaine Bent who wasn't Killa from DFC, then it wouldn't have to be real and I could go back to normal. Maybe I don't have what it takes to be a detective after all. Maybe it's too risky.

Scene Twenty-five

Harri *and* **Dean** *are confronted by the* **Dell Farm Crew** *at School.*

Dizzy   What's up pussy boy?

Clipz   I heard you failed the first test – That's moist rude boey

Killa   This youth's weak man.

Harri   I wanted to be a bomb. I wanted to knock them all down.

X-Fire   Don't worry Ghana – I'll think of something easier for you next time, you'll be alright. What you got for me Tin Tin?

Dean *is frozen with fear.*

Dean   I ain't got nothing.

Killa   Don't lie to us man – what's in your pockets – Empty them out.

Dean *reluctantly starts to empty his pockets.*

Dean   I've got a quid, that's it. I need it.

Dizzy   Yeah well, shit happens innit.

Dizzy *snatches* **Dean***'s quid.*

Dean *is stunned and upset.*

Dean   F – ing hell man –

Dizzy   Don't try and front me you little bitch – Fix your face or I'll knock you out – Can you believe this facety youth. Bounce

Dean *scurries off.*

Robbing Mr Frimpong.

Harri   It was me and X-Fire, Dizzy and Killa. They were going to crash the target and I was going to run with the prize.

Killa   Don't worry blud, you just stay with us, yeah! If it looks like it's getting F –ed up, I'll give you the sign – then you just get out of there – got it?

Harri   Got it –

X-Fire *and* **Dizzy** *leave to scope out the area.*

Harri   The sign is a nod – I'll only fail the misson if I split before the end. X-Fire was in charge of picking the target. It had to be somebody weaker, that way you could knock them down easily. They couldn't fight back, it was quicker. We had to keep our backs to the camera until X-Fire found a target.

X-Fire   Here we go – This one'll do.

Mr Frimpong *is alone and walking with a bag of shopping.*

Harri   That's when I knew Mr Frimpong was the target. I felt sick all over again.

X-Fire   Let's do this shit – Go!

Harri *pulls his coat over his head.*

Harri   We ran –

X -Fire and Killa ran together. I just followed them.

I couldn't stop. I just ran as fast as I could.

Mr Frimpong *is knocked to the floor.*

There is a struggle and **Mr Frimpong** *is set upon.*

Harri   It wasn't me – it wasn't me – it wasn't me! [I just said it inside my head]

X-Fire *has a scarf over his face.*

X-Fire   Give it up you old bastard or I'll shank you.

Killa   Wet him up blud –

X-Fire   He ain't worth it still –

He searches **Mr Frimpong***'s pockets and gets his wallet.*

Harri   *If you fail two missions you'll never get in. I turned around and ran as fast as I could.*

X-Fire   Where the F – you going?

Scene Twenty-six

At the Flat.

Miguita *is sat on one end of the sofa.*

Harri *is sat on the other end trying to ignore* **Miquita**.

Lydia *is painting her fingernails.*

Dean *is sat awkwardly nearby.*

Harri Poppy doesn't need to wear make-ups because she already is beautiful. Miquita and Chanelle and all the others only have to wear it because they're ugly underneath. At afternoon Registration Poppy gave me a letter. I wasn't allowed to show it to anybody else.

Harri *opens and reads the letter with a confused expression.*

Do you like me?

Yes or No

I just have to tick the box. I have to give the letter back to Poppy. I don't know what will happen when I give it back.

Harri *writes on the piece of paper.*

Asweh, I hope it was the right answer

Miquita *touches up her green eyeshadow.*

Miquita *is putting her cherry lipstick on.*

Miquita Are you ready for me then? Did you brush your teeth? No, I'm only joking, I know you're clean. You're a sweet boy innit.

Harri Miquita's going to teach me how to kiss. Miquita has sucked off a hundred boys, she knows all the best ways to do it. If I know how to kiss properly then Poppy will never cut me for another boy.

Lydia *laughing.*

Lydia I want a lover – Not a Casanova

Harri Gowayou –

Lydia We will love every day – You will be my lover

Harri Shut up – I go sound you –

Miquita Just hold still, Juicy Fruit – Relax –

Miquita *pushes and squeezes* **Harri** *down on the sofa.*

Miquita Open your mouth man – Yeah, that's it. Relax man – You're gonna like it, I promise.

Miquita *slowly leans in towards* **Harri**.

Harri   Everything went proper slow. I could feel Miquita's boob was touching my arm, then she ...

Sound of **Miquita** *kissing* **Harri**.

Harri   It was quite soft. It was even not too bad until I felt her tongue go in.

Nnnnngggtnggg, yudiiingsaanythnnnnngabouuutnnnng –

Harri's *flailing arms and legs are seen coming from the sofa.*

Miquita *stops.*

Miquita   What was that?

Harri   You didn't say anything about tongues –

Miquita   But everyone likes the tongue – You gotta learn the best way or there's no point – Just go with it.

Lydia   They're only year 7, they don't need to know about tongues –

Miquita   Shut up man – what would you know? Just let me do my work innit.

Do you want your brother to be a batty boy?

Miquita *slowly moves down to continue kissing* **Harri**.

Harri *holds on to the back of the sofa.*

The sound of **Miquita** *kissing* **Harri** *is heard.*

Harri   I just thought about Poppy. I made her yellow fill me up like the sun.

Lydia   Miquita

Miquita   Just relax man – Give me it.

Miquita *pinches* **Harri**'s *hand to make him let go of the sofa.*

Harri   She took it and put it down her pant. I could feel hair on my fingers. I swear by God, I wanted to be sick. She peeled my fingers apart and stuck one up her toto. It felt wet and rubbery. She got another finger and another finger and she made my hand go up and down.

Miquita *started licking her lips.*

Harri   Stoppih – Lydia – Hellllpe – Gehheroff

Lydia   He's had enough – He keeps holding his breath.

Miquita   I'll say when he's had enough, what are you gonna do Chlamydia? Stop wriggling man. I thought you wanted to learn.

Harri   I changed my mind. Get off me –

Harri *musters the strength to push* **Miquita** *off him.*

Miquita *looks overwhelmed and breathless.*

Miquita *jeans are open.*

Miquita   Not bad for a beginner – Don't lick my teeth tough, girls don't like it. Wanna try again?

Harri   Go away – I'm not doing it anymore – just piss off. It was a bad idea – Stupid witch – You're not even funny.

Miquita   We ain't finished yet, that was just the first lesson innit. Did I make your willy go hard? Did you get a funny feeling down there?

Harri   No –

Lydia   Don't say that, he's too young. Just leave him alone.

Miquita   Who are you – his mum? Just cause you're frigid, don't mean everyone's like you. You lot are so f – ing lame man.

Lydia   At least my boyfriend's not a murderer –

The room becomes silent and tense.

Miquita   What did you say?

Harri   (*nervously*) You shouldn't let them burn you.

Miquita   What?

Lydia   You should just tell him to stop. Look at your hands, how could you let someone do that to you? That's just weak.

Miquita *buttons up her jeans.*

Miquita   Who you calling weak? I ain't anyone you can chat to anyhow –

Lydia   Just go home Miquita – We don't want you here anymore.

Miquita   Am I s'posed to care? You're just a stupid little bitch.

Miquita *leaves quietly.*

Harri *locks the door behind* **Miquita**.

There's a packet of Oreos on a table.

Harri *opens it and offers one to* **Lydia** *and* **Dean**.

Harri   The first one is always the tastiest.

Scene Twenty-seven

Lydia's birthday.

Mamma *sings Happy Birthday as she carries in a home-made cake with candles.*

Lydia *has a red Samsung Galaxy given to her by* **Auntie Sonia**.

Auntie Sonia *has a bandage over her nose and the skin around her eyes is bruised.*

Mamma   I don't want you taking it to school.

Lydia   I'll only use it for emergencies. It's for you really, so you can know where I am the whole time. It's safer like that.

Harri   Liar – she only wants it so she can talk rudeness to Miquita.

Lydia   How! No I don't –

Mamma   What rudeness?

Lydia   Nothing –

Harri   All about kissing boys –

Auntie Sonia   I didn't want you to be left out Harri so I got you this –

Auntie Sonia *presents* **Harri** *with an unwrapped remote control car.*

Harri   Ah – It's so hutious – Auntie Sonia – What happened to your nose?

Mamma   Yes – how did you hurt it – tell us?

Auntie Sonia   It was my own stupid fault. I was reaching for my suitcase with your presents off the top of the wardrobe – I was looking for a dress – It slid off and hit me right on the nose. Broke it like that. I saw stars.

Lydia   Silly thing –

Mamma   You should be more careful –

Auntie Sonia   I know –

Julius *enters drinking a bottle of beer.*

Auntie Sonia *goes quiet.*

Julius   That's better –

Julius *sits next to* **Auntie Sonia.**

Auntie Sonia   I'll put some credit in there for you – Pay as you go.

Lydia *takes a photo.*

Julius   Did you ask for my permission before you took a photo?

Auntie Sonia   Julius – she was only –

Julius   I wasn't taking to you -

Lydia   I – I didn't –

Julius   Show me –

Lydia *shows* **Julius** *the photo.*

Julius   It's too dark you should delete it –

Lydia   Yes that's what I thought

Mamma   Harri you should go and get Lydia's package –

Harri   Yes – (*he runs off*)

Julius   Take another one –

Lydia   Really –

Julius   Of course – Come Mamma –

Mamma *reluctantly sits on the other side of* **Julius**.

Lydia   Say cheese

All three   Cheese

Lydia *takes the photo.*

Julius *does a big dirty laugh.*

Julius's *phone rings.*

Julius   Hello – What did I say to you about calling on this number –

Julius *goes outside to take the call.*

Auntie Sonia   Let see –

Lydia *shows the image to* **Auntie Sonia**.

Harri *returning.*

Harri   It's heavy

Lydia   Hurry up –

Harri   I'm bringing it – Keep you hair on –

Mamma   Don't vex her – Or I'll give your piece of cake to the pigeons.

Harri   The postman gave the box to me. I was going to keep it at first.

Lydia   Hands off – I go sound you.

Harri   In your dreams –

Harri *picks up* **Lydia***'s phone and takes photos of her opening her birthday present. There are two CDs from Abena, one of Michael Jackson, and one of Kwaw Kese. There are gold hoop earrings from Grandma Ama.* **Harri** *bites the earrings to test the quality.*

Lydia   Get my earrings out of your mouth, you're getting spit all on them.

Harri   Do you want me to test them or not?

Lydia   Not –

Out of the box **Lydia** *also pulls out a picture of her baby sister* **Agnes***'s hand. There is also a small wooden figurine of a dancer from* **Papa***.*

Lydia *starts to cry.*

Auntie Sonia   Don't Cry –

Harri   I'll have it if you don't want it. I can swap it at school. I might even get a disco watch for it.

Lydia   Don't disturb –

Harri   Why be like that?

Mamma   She's missing her Papa, that's all. Don't vex her.

Harri   Don't be sad. It's your birthday. Your nose is all snotty –

Lydia   Shut up –

Mamma   Harrison, just leave her –

Harri   I had to make Lydia laugh. If I didn't make her laugh the whole day would be finished

Harri   Come on, sweetheart – Chin up –

No response from **Lydia**.

Nothing – Not even a tiny smile

No response from **Lydia**.

Turn your frown upside down – You know it makes sense.

No response from **Lydia**.

Nothing again

No response from **Lydia**.

Harri   You are my sunshine, my only sunshine. You make me happy when tings are gay.

Mamma   Harrison – Enough with the gay –

Lydia   Stop it – (*suppressing a smile*)

Harri   Rub a dub dub, no need to blub – I love you from the heart of my bottom.

Lydia   Stop it – (*smiling*)

Harri   Got you – I win –

Lydia *laughs out loud.*

Harri   Do you want my presents? You have to follow me, it's outside.

Lydia   Gowayou – I'm not falling for another trick.

Harri   It's not a trick, I promise –

Lydia *looks curiously at* **Mamma**.

Mamma   Don't look at me, I have nothing to do with this –

Harri   Just come on, scaredy cat –

Lydia   Where are we going?

Harri   You'll see – Just trust me –

Harri *and* **Lydia** *leave.*

Mamma   You don't have to go anywhere. You can stay here until you find somewhere else.

Auntie Sonia   And have Julius coming around here making trouble for everybody? I don't want to get you any more involved that you are already –

Mamma   It's too late for that – It has been ever since I took his money –

Auntie Sonia   I should never have told you about him.

Mamma   How else would I have made it here? Should I have planted a plane ticket tree? I'd still be at home putting coins in a milo tin, ten pesewa here, fifty there. I made the choice, nobody forced me. I did it for me, for these children. As long as I pay my debt they're safe and sound. They grow up to reach further than I could ever carry them. I'm here now, let me help you. Just tell me what you need. You can't keep running forever –

Lydia *searches unsuccessfully for her present.*

Harri *looks on with excitement.*

Harri   It felt brutal.

Lydia   Just give me my present and let's go – Where is it?

Harri   Right in front of you – The cement was still wet. The council man was gone for his chop. If you were going to do it, it had to be now. You couldn't plan it any better.

Lydia   What am I supposed to be doing here?

Harri   Just jump – It'll be brutal – Your footprints will get struck and when it dries they'll be trapped forever – Then the ramp and the whole tower will belong to us. You have to jump quite hard though. You have to mean it.

Lydia   That's stupid – I'm not jumping in that –

Harri   Go on – It will only take one second – You put your footprints in it and I'll write your name next to them so everybody knows. We'll both do it. I'll go first.

Harri *positions himself, before jumping with both feet into the cement.* **Harri** *squats pushing the weight of his body down to make better indentation in the cement.*

Lydia   It looks like you're doing a shit –

Harri   It's the best way – Just watch me – 1, 2, 3, 4, 5, 6, 7, 8, 9 10

Harri *does a little twist and jumps back out of the cement.*

Harri   Look you can see the Diadora signs under my trainers –

Lydia   You're so lame –

Harri   Just do it, lazy face – You can't give a present back if somebody plans it for you. It's like saying you hate them.

Lydia   Ok – Ok –

Lydia *jumps next to* **Harri***'s footprint.*

She squats into a similar positions as **Harri***.*

Her lips move as she quietly counts to ten.

Harri   Now give it a little twist –

Lydia   I'm twisting – I'm twisting –

Lydia *struggles to jump back out.*

Her feet are stuck and unbalanced, she nearly falls.

Lydia *screams.*

Lydia   Help me – Help me –

Harri   Don't panic, I've got you –

Harri *pulls* **Lydia** *out of the cement.*

Lydia   Quick and write the names before it goes too dry –

Harri *drops down to write both their names under the footprints.*

Harri   Asweh, it looked bo-styles.

Lydia *is smiling in delirious delight.*

Harri   Happy birthday – I told you you'd love it.

Scene Twenty-eight

Toy Car.

Harri *quietly and cautiously knocks on a door.*

Harri   I kept looking at Jordan's door. I was waiting for it to open.

The door opens.

Jordan *walks out to see* **Harri** *playing with a remote control car.*

Jordan *is envious but doesn't speak.*

Harri *intentionally crashes into things.*

Jordan   Give us a go –

Harri *stops and looks at* **Jordan** *then back to the car and continues playing.*

Harri   In a minute –

Silence.

Jordan   Come on man, give us a go. You've had it ages.

Harri   You'll break it –

Jordan   No I won't, I'm a wicked driver – I never crash –

Harri   We're not even friends anymore –

Jordan   Who says? Come on man.

Harri   Two more minutes –

Jordan   One minute. I'll show you how to make it flip over, It's well sick –

Harri   This is the bit I'd been waiting for. I had to make him want it proper bad. I had to make him beg. That way when I took it away it would hurt even more. I wanted to punish him

Silence.

Jordan *is getting restless.*

Harri *wants to laugh but stifles the urge.*

Harri   I can't, I've got to go in now. My dinner's ready.

Harri *picks up the car and goes inside.*

The sound of **Harri** *shutting his front door is heard.*

Jordan *is left alone.*

Jordan *returns inside.*

Scene Twenty-nine

At School.

Miquita *and* **Chanelle** *fight.*

Harri   There was a ruckus at lunch time. It was the best one so far. Nobody knew why they were fighting.

Miquita   You f – ing skank – You ain't gonna tell shit.

Miquita *grabs* **Chanelle***'s hair and an uprooted patch of hair comes out in her hand.*

Miquita *blows the hair out of her hands.*

Spectators scream and jump out of the way of the descending strands of hair.

Chanelle *folds herself down and aims her whole weight into* **Miquita***'s midriff.* **Miquita** *is thrown back and nearly breaks out of the circle of spectators, but the circle throws her back in at* **Chanelle***.*

Miquita *tries to dig her fingers into* **Miquita***'s eyes.*

Chanelle *uses her strength to push* **Miquita** *back.*

Miquita *lunges back in and pulls* **Chanelle** *by her ears.*

Chanelle   My earrings!

The girls stop fighting.

Miquita *lets go of* **Chanelle**, *both the girls are huffing and puffing; they circle each other as* **Chanelle** *takes off her earrings and puts them in her pockets.*

As she does so **Miquita** *lunges back in and gets* **Chanelle** *in a head lock.*

Chanelle *restricted and unable to see struggles to free herself by stamping on* **Miquita**'s *feet.*

Harri   You actually thought they were going to kill each other. You wanted them to stop. It wasn't funny anymore.

Everybody   Kill her – Kill her – Bang her up – Slump her rude gal –

Harri   Some of the **Dell Farm Crew** were there

Dell Farm Crew *apart from* **Killa** *are laughing.*

Harri   Dizzy was taking a picture on his phone.

Everyone else get their phones out.

Dizzy   Rarse – You're gonna die bitch –

Killa *looked worried for* **Miquita**.

Killa *starts to leave.*

X-Fire *grabs him back.*

X-Fire   Where you going man? Don't you want to watch you girl defend it – You made this shit –

Killa   F – off man – I didn't make nothing –

Dizzy   Throw her through the tuck-shop window man –

Miquita *starts pulling* **Chanelle** *towards the window.*

Chanelle *is resisting and trying to pull the other way.*

Miquita   This is what you get – You best keep your mouth shut bitch –

Teachers *arrive blowing a whistle and bursting through the circle. On the ground there is an excessive array of broken colourful fingernails, patches of hair/weave extensions and earrings.*

Teacher   Break it up – Miquita, headteacher's office now –

Miquita   I didn't do nothing – she started it – I was just defending myself –

The spectators pick up various objects off the floor and laugh, chasing each other with the cartoonish debris.

Scene Thirty

Wallet in the Playground.

Harri *and* **Dean** *are lying on their backs in the middle of the basketball court.*

Harri   Are you feeling anything yet?

Dean   Yeah f – ing stupid – It's not working man. Come on let's go.

Harri   Keep trying – Pretend like you're the Dead Boy. Pretend like you can feel what he felt and see what he saw. It works better if you concentrate.

The Dead Boy was brilliant at basketball. One time he scored a basket at from one in a million shot. You'll never see one like that again. Everybody said it was a fluke but he just smiled like he planned it all along.

X-Fire   F – ing poser – anyone could've made that shot –

Dead boy   Go on then, Let's see you make it.

X-Fire   F – off, man don't try and front me or you'll get moved to.

Killa   Watch your mouth or you'll get slumped –

Dead boy   Easy now children – Play nice yeah?

Harri   I was watching from outside. I could see it all happening through the fence.

X-Fire *pushes the* **Dead Boy**.

Killa *also pushes him.*

The **Dead Boy** *pushes* **Killa** *with enough force to knock him back onto the floor.*

As **Killa** *gets back up he is restrained by the rest of the DFC.*

In the back of **Killa**'s *jeans you can see the handle of the screwdriver.*

Killa *jostles to get to the* **Dead Boy**.

The **Dead Boy** *taunts* **Killa**.

All the other players become spectators.

Killa *and the DFC leave.*

The **Dead Boy** *continues playing basketball.*

Dean   I'm telling you, I'm not getting anything –

Harri   It's because he didn't know you, his spirit doesn't trust if you're friendly or not. It's ok, spirit, he's with me. We only want to help.

X-Fire   What you two batty boys doing? You been eating retard sandwiches again?

Clipz *and* **Dizzy** *circle* **Dean** *and* **Harri**.

Killa   Don't you know you're trespassing? You'll have to pay the tax now straight. How much you got?

Dean   Nothing –

Killa   Don't make me hurt you – empty your pockets –

Killa *makes* **Dean** *empty his pockets –*

Killa *retrieves 63p and two Black Jacks.*

Killa   What about your trainers?

Dean   What about them?

Killa   Just take them off before I batter you – I ain't messing about man.

Dean *takes off his trainers.*

Dean*'s socks have an elaborate funny cartoon illustration on them.*

Dean *empties out his trainers – Nothing to hide.*

X-Fire   What about you Ghana? What you hiding?

Harri   Nothing –

Harri *holds his pocket with the dead boy's wallet.*

Killa   What you got there?

Killa *pulls back* **Harri***'s arm.*

Harri *tries to resist by digging his hand further down into his pocket.*

Killa *stamps on* **Harri***'s feet.*

Killa *digs his hands into* **Harri***'s pocket and gets the wallet out.*

Killa   What's this? There better be some cash in here –

Killa *opens the wallet and the dead boy's picture falls out.*

The wallet is empty.

Killa *see the picture on the floor.*

He enters the basketball court and picks up the picture.

Silence.

Killa *studies the picture.*

Killa*'s face stiffens.*

X-Fire   What is it man?

Killa   Where'd you get this?

Dean We found it –

Miquita (*tries to comfort* **Killa**) It's alright – It's only a picture, it don't mean nothing –

Killa (*to* **Miquita**) What the f – do you know? You don't know shit.

Miquita I'm just saying babes –

Killa Get off me –

Killa *pushes* **Miquita** *away.*

Dean *puts his trainers back on.*

Killa *is transfixed by the dead boy's picture.*

X-Fire F – ing sort it out man – just get rid of it, yeah? Just fucking go –

Killa What if I don't want to? This shit's gone too far man – It's over –

X-Fire I say when it's over – Don't pussy out on us now, You got us in this shit. Just give me the fucking thing and go –

X-Fire *takes the picture from* **Killa** *and jostles him and kicks him to leave.*

Miquita *followed behind* **Killa***.*

Killa *pushes her away.*

Killa *is in tears.*

As he runs away his elbows stick out in a feminine way.

X-Fire *burns the* **Dead Boy***'s picture with his lighter.*

X-Fire Harvey – Dizzy cover the gate man. They ain't going anywhere –

X-Fire *reaches into the back of his trousers.*

X-Fire *puts his hood up.*

Lydia Get away from him – I called the police.

Lydia *is filming with her phone.*

X-Fire   Get her –

Harri   Run –

They give chase.

Dean *and* **Harri** *quickly dodge* **X-Fire** *as he is distracted and exit the now unmanned gate.*

X-Fire   I'm gonna fucking kill you –

Harri, Lydia *and* **Dean** *are reunited.*

Lydia   The library – Quick –

Dean *and* **Harri** *are breathless.*

Harri   We ran into the big library, we had to be safe there.

Lydia   I got everything on my phone –

Lydia *shows* **Dean** *and* **Harri** *some of the footage.*

Dean   Don't delete it, will you –

Lydia   I won't – What have you been messing in?

Harri   We were only doing our duty –

Lydia   Mamma go sound you –

Dean   Now we know Killa must have jooked up the Dead Boy – He had all the signs of guilt –

Harri   Now he knows we know –

Lydia   I thought X-Fire was different – he's just the same as the rest –

Scene Thirty-one

Fire.

The playground is burning.

Harri   You could feel the fire for miles. Somebody set the swings on fire. The climbing frame was on fire as well. The fire was very hot. Everybody went to watch the playground die.

Mr Tomlin   I can feel myself getting lost in this big smoke, it's suffocating the amount of hate around I'm thinking it's time to migrate, if I have kids they're growing up in the countryside away from these urban estates.

Lydia   I have the whole thing on my phone. Everything!.. Crossfire… the picture of the Dead Boy … him burning the picture. He knows! Maybe it wasn't him. Maybe he just got caught in the crossfire of madness or maybe, maybe he's just a murderer.

Chorus (2x)   I can feel the pain, I can feel the pain
It was burning, It was burning

X-Fire   I've been around these streets long enough to know that everyone has secrets. I gotta keep my head strong, stay calm cause Killa's near gone losing his back bone, but I'm the king of this throne I've got to get back that phone so we don't all end up bang up doing a long stretch till we're old and alone.

Killa   They call me Killa, so imma take the name
They call me Killa so imma embrace the shame
I blaze and rage for the status
If Harri snakes I'll be the bate for the feds gazes.
It's a hell in front of us
Futures dead full of no hope and loose lips stuffed full of curses
And seeing as everyone, bedrins, *Jesus* even Mum, has lied to me
Imma lay claim to a rage which will end this path, end the guilt
and end this name

Miquita   Things are getting peak
Killa needs to know I won't speak
He wants to retreat disappearing from me like a cruel trick
Times like this I know he needs me
Love is a hype when he's just your type
But when he just ain't got no time it feels like a crime

Jordan   Black smoke from the swing. And the fires blazing amazing.

But I can feel me getting hot, so what?

Mum wouldn't care if it took me or if someone jooked me.

I should lead the fire to the school, I'd be cool ... ow!

The fires getting hot, so what, no loss ... Mamma wouldn't care if it took me, or if someone jooked me. I should throw Harri in there, prick, quick, the fires hot, so what, no loss,

Mother   You will never understand the trouble it took us to get here, I was sold a lie to get to the promised land. Now all I see, all I see, Now all I see, all I see, is fire, fire. Where is my son? I said where is my son? All I see is fire, where is my son?

Scene Thirty-two

Never Normal Girl *is outside the flats drawing on the pavement outside the flats with coloured chalk.*

Harri   Some superheroes are from another planet. Some of them were made in a factory. Some of them were born normal but they had an accident that gave them their powers. It's usually because of radiation. I didn't even think Never Normal Girl could draw. Who is that? It's very good –

Never Normal Girl   She lives on the other side of the world in a big house with a big garden with fairies that make her pretty dresses and make her food no one else has ever tasted. At night she puts on her special, special clothes and goes out to help people. She's my doppelganger –

Harri   What is that?

Never Normal Girl   She looks like me –

Harri   You have a twin sister –

Never Normal Girl   No – she just looks like me but we're not related –

Harri   So you've never met – but how do you know about her?

Never Normal Girl   I just do – I can feel it – She's looking for me –

Mamma   Harrison where have you been – Did you not see the fire – I want you home now now – Oh hello – Is that Poppy?

Harri *irritated and embarrassed.*

Harri   No Mamma – this is not Poppy

Mamma   Oh Ok – lets go –

Harri *being dragged by* **Mamma**.

Harri *shouts.*

Harri   When I get back – from school tomorrow – You can show me more

Never Normal Girl   Ok –

Harri *breaks away from* **Mamma** *and returns.*

Harri   Just to let you know – I don't think you smell –

Mamma   Harrison –

Scene Thirty-three

A swarm of excited school children sweep past **Harri**.

Dean *sneaks up behind* **Harri**.

Dean *stops, noticing something on* **Harri***'s backpack.*

Harri   Me and Dean and Lydia are walking to school together this morning for extra security.

Dean   What's that?

Harri   How! – You scared me –

Dean   You've got initials on your bag – in tipex

Lydia   Have you been graffitting you bag – Mamma go sound you – she's not going to buy you a new one –

Harri   I don't want a new bag –

Dean   P. M plus H. O then I. F. S. T – what's that, some kind of code?

Harri   None of your business –

Dean   H. O must be you – Harri Opoku – Whose P. M? Peter – Patrick – Pauuuuuuu – Paul – Patrick –

Harri   Poppy – It stands for Poppy Morgan –

Dean   I know I just wanted to watch your face twist into knots – Poppy Morgan that's new –

Harri   No – Yes – But we've liked each other for a long time – She fills me with yellow –

Dean   You like her – You want to kiss her – You want to marry her – and have babies – You want to toasts her (*puts his hands together*) and make her (*he claps his hands together*) piiiinnnnnggggg – ping – ping –

Lydia   I don't have time for your childish games – What are we going to do? I can't live the whole summer in fear for my life like this

Dean   I don't want to be terrorised by the DFC anymore either – We have to do something –

Harri   We solved the case that's why they're after us – It's just what they bad guys have to do –

Dean   I'm not going on the run – I only have a bus pass, you need at least two passports

Harri   We have two passports –

Lydia   I think convincing Mamma will be difficult – She has a good job.

Dean   If Dizzy tries to rob me again I'll have to do something – (*shows a penknife*)

Harri   No you can't – I don't want to come to your funeral – We just have to go to the police with all our evidence –

Dean   When? We can't do it today –

Harri   Tomorrow morning we can tell our mums so they can take us, then the police will believe us more –

Dean   We might get a tour before they give us our rewards –

Harri   I hope they show us the torture room –

Dean   They'll stick Killa's head in a bucket of water until he admits it –

Harri   What will you buy with your reward?

Dean   I'll buy a new bike – You'll have the same one in a different colour and we'll ride it around London, to the eye, to the palace –

Harri   and the dinosaur museum

Dean   we can hide in the T-Rex ribs, then we can jump out when they close up for the night and we'll have the place to ourselves –

Harri   It'll be hutious –

Lydia   What about me – I have the video on my phone – I should get something too –

Dean   Err –

Harri   You get Papa, Grandma Ama and

Lydia   Agnes –

Harri   We'll buy them all tickets so that we can all be a family again like before –

Kylie   You know what day it is?

Harri   It's not your birthday is it –

Dean   Already – Again?

Kylie   No it's not my birthday –

Harri   Then what day is it?

Kylie   It's the last day of school – holiday bitches – We're free –

Kylie *pulls bag of flour from her bag and throws it at* **Harri**, **Dean** *and* **Lydia**.

All three are stunned and **Kylie** *runs off laughing.*

Kylie   Every bitch for themselves – bitches –

Scene Thirty-three b

Chaos ensues and students have their school shirts signed. Coloured chalk and flour are thrown and some students have poppers; using makeshift bottles with holes as water pistols they squirt at one another. It's an impromptu school party, neither students nor teachers are safe.

Students   Started from the bottom now we're here –

Student   Where's the bitches?

Student   Fuck the Police –

Student   Me love you long time –

Student   Virgins –

Student   Nobody cares – Get high –

Student   Marvin is peng –

Student   I'm the only gay in the village

Student   Summer summer time – Summer time –

Student   I stink of jizz

Student   We're all made of stars –

Student   Cheese tits –

Student   Big words –

Student   See you at the Job Centre –

Student Everybody's a cunt except me

Teacher Live your dream –

Student Get rich or die trying –

Student Spoon –

Scene Thirty-four

Harri *stands alone.*

Harri *seems to have a secret he's desperately trying to contain.*

Harri *is blushing.*

Harri *can't hold it in any longer.*

Harri Poppy just kissed me – right on the lips … (*privately whispers to the audience*) It felt lovely – She's my girlfriend now –

Harri *celebrates with a dance.*

Harri *takes in a big breath and gets himself into a running start position.*

I am going to count how long it takes to get home.

Harri *starts to move his arms as if warming up.*

I could feel my blood getting stronger. I started running. I ran fast. I ran down the hill and through the tunnel.

Harri *shouts.*

Poppy I love you –

The tunnel echoes loudly.

I ran past the real church.
I ran past the jubilee centre.
I ran past the CCTV camera.
I let it snap me for luck.
I ran past the pigeons and pretended they said hello to me.

Pigeons I love you.

I ran past the playground and the dead climbing frame.

Harri *runs even faster.*

I was running super fast.
I ran so fast my feet were just a blur.
I was going to break the world record.
My lips still tickled from where Poppy's kiss had been.
I ran past a tree in a cage.

Tree I love you –

I could see the flats.
The stair would be safe.
I ran through the tunnel.
My breath was nearly gone, I couldn't get the words out
anymore.

Aaaaaaaaaaaahhhhhhhhhhhhhhhhhh!
Asweh, It was the best echo ever.

Harri *breaths heavily.*

The sweat was itching on my face.
It felt less than seven minutes, it felt like only five. I did it.

A hooded figure approaches **Harri** *and stabs him swiftly.*

I didn't see him. He came out of nowhere.
I couldn't get out of the way, he was too fast.
I should have seen him but I wasn't paying attention.
You need eyes in the back of your head.
I've never been chooked before –

Harri *falls to the bottom of the stairs holding his belly.*

I could smell the piss....

I didn't want to die.

(*struggles for voice*) Mamma

Mamma was at work. Papa was too far away he'd never hear it.

I would tell the police I only saw the handle for one second, It could have be green or brown.

Harri *closes his eyes.*

I wanted to laugh but it hurt too much.

Harri *opens his eyes.*

It could be a dream except (*looks down at his stomach*) there was a bigger puddle and it wasn't piss it was me.

My blood is darker than I thought.

I hope Lydia tells Agnes my story, the one about the man on the plane with the fake leg.

She'll love that one.

I can see your face Agnes and your tiny fingers.
All babies look the same.

Harri *takes in one last large gasping breath.*
Eyes wide.

Blackout